W9-BFI-627

976.6
HEI

AMERICA the BEAUTIFUL
OKLAHOMA

By Ann Heinrichs

Consultants

Rita Geiger, Social Studies Specialist, Oklahoma State Department of Education, Oklahoma City

Carl Oliver, Ed.D., Professor of Education, Social Studies Specialist, The University of Tulsa

C.W. West, Muskogee Historian, author of *Only in Oklahoma*

Robert L. Hillerich, Ph.D., Bowling Green State University, Bowling Green, Ohio

CHILDRENS PRESS®
CHICAGO

An oil pump in Osage County

Project Editor: Joan Downing
Assistant Editor: Shari Joffe
Design Director: Margrit Fiddle
Typesetting: Graphic Connections, Inc.
Engraving: Liberty Photoengraving

Childrens Press®, Chicago
Copyright ©1989 by Regensteiner Publishing Enterprises, Inc.
All rights reserved. Published simultaneously in Canada.
Printed in the United States of America.
1 2 3 4 5 6 7 8 9 10 R 98 97 96 95 94 93 92 91 90 89

Library of Congress Cataloging-in-Publication Data

Heinrichs, Ann.
    America the beautiful. Oklahoma / by Ann Heinrichs.
        p.   cm.
    Includes index.
    Summary: Introduces this central state that has been a
"Dust Bowl," Indian Territory, oil rich, and a promised
land to settlers.
    ISBN 0-516-00482-4
    1. Oklahoma—Juvenile literature.   [1.   Oklahoma.]
I.   Title.
F694.3.H44   1988   88-11743
976.6—dc19   CIP
                                                    AC

The Pioneer
Woman statue,
Ponca City

TABLE OF CONTENTS

Chapter 1

AN INTRODUCTION
TO THE SOONER STATE

AN INTRODUCTION TO THE SOONER STATE

According to an Oklahoma folk tale, an old-timer was showing his little patch of farmland to a visitor from "up north." Pretty soon a spindly-legged roadrunner sped across their path.

"What bird is that?" asked the visitor.

"Why, that's one of our native birds," the old-timer replied. "That there's a bird o' paradise!"

"If that's a bird o' paradise," the visitor concluded, looking around at the scrubby vegetation and the red clay soil, "seems to me he's a long way from home!"

If the visitor could have seen the rest of Oklahoma, he might have caught a glimpse of that paradise the old-timer knew and loved. The land was a nature-lover's paradise even in prehistoric times, when Indians fished the sparkling rivers and tilled the bounteous soil. By 1889, word had spread. Promoters known as "Boomers" were calling it the "promised land." Eager "Sooners" rushed to stake early claims. This era gave Oklahoma its two nicknames, the Sooner State and the Boomer State.

Today's Oklahoma reflects the spirit of the Old West as well as a love of the land. Its people work with the same energy and industry that has seen Oklahomans through decades of hardship. For vacationers, the state is a paradise of sparkling lakes and breathtaking vistas. These lines from the state song truly echo Oklahomans' pride:

> We know we belong to the land
> And the land we belong to is grand!

Chapter 2
THE LAND

THE LAND

Oklahoma resembles a deep-dish frying pan or skillet, with the pan's handle extending out to the west. Although it is not the only state with a "panhandle," this feature makes Oklahoma easy to spot on a map.

GEOGRAPHY AND TOPOGRAPHY

Oklahoma lies just south of the geographical center of the United States. Kansas and a part of Colorado form the northern border of the state; Arkansas and Missouri lie to the east; Texas forms the southern border; and Texas and New Mexico form the western borders.

Because of its Panhandle, Oklahoma's overall width is more than twice its depth. Ranking eighteenth among all states in size, Oklahoma measures 230 miles (370 kilometers) from north to south and 464 miles (747 kilometers) from its eastern edge to the tip of the Panhandle. The Panhandle itself is only about 34 miles (55 kilometers) wide.

Topographically, the state slopes from northwest to southeast. Black Mesa, in the Panhandle, is the highest point, measuring 4,973 feet (1,516 meters) above sea level. The lowest point lies along the Little River in the far southeast corner, at 287 feet (87 meters) above sea level.

Wheat harvesting on a farm in the fertile Red Bed Plains, the state's largest land region

LAND REGIONS

Three of the great land regions of the United States meet in Oklahoma. These are the Interior Plains, stretching east from the Rocky Mountains; the Coastal Plain, reaching up through Texas from the Gulf of Mexico; and the Interior (or Ozark-Ouachita) Highlands, rising between the Interior Plains and the Coastal Plain.

Within Oklahoma are ten subregions, offering a variety of landscapes—high plains, low plains, craggy and eroded rock formations, and fertile valleys.

Seven of the state's subregions lie within the Interior Plains: the High Plains, the Gypsum Hills, the Red Bed Plains, the Sandstone Hills, the Prairie Plains, the Wichita Mountains, and the Arbuckle Mountains. The Ozark Plateau and the Ouachita Mountains are part of the Interior Highlands. The Red River Region is part of the Coastal Plain.

Northwestern Oklahoma, including the Panhandle, is the High Plains region. Grasslands here rise toward Black Mesa, on the tip of the Panhandle. To the east, the sparkling gypsum of the Glass Mountains highlights the Gypsum Hills region. Down the center of the state, from north to south, lie the fertile, rolling Red Bed Plains, the state's largest land area. East of these plains, also stretching from north to south, are the forested hills, oil fields, and farms of the Sandstone Hills. East of the Sandstone Hills lies the farmland of the Arkansas Valley, the Prairie Plains. The granite peaks of the Wichita Mountains rise in the southwest, with lakes and a wildlife refuge on lower ground. In the south-central plains stand the craggy, eroded granite and limestone formations of the Arbuckle Mountains.

In the northeast are the hills, streams, and valleys of the Ozark Plateau. The Ouachita Mountain area of the southeast is a region of forests and rough sandstone ridges.

South of the Ouachitas, along the southern border, is the fertile Red River Region, part of the Gulf Coastal Plain.

RIVERS

Oklahoma lies in the western Mississippi River Valley, which means its nearly 23,000 miles (37,015 kilometers) of rivers and streams flow to the east. The Red River forms Oklahoma's southern border, continues east through Louisiana, and empties into the Mississippi River. The Arkansas River cuts across the northeastern part of the state, flows through Arkansas, and eventually joins the Mississippi as well.

Tributaries of the Arkansas River branch out across the entire state. These include the North Canadian and South Canadian rivers, which cross almost the full width of Oklahoma; and the

11

Canoeing on the Illinois River, one of the many tributaries of the Arkansas

Cimarron River, which drains the north-central region and touches the western tip of the Panhandle. Other major tributaries of the Arkansas River are the Verdigris, the Illinois, and the Grand (Neosho) rivers.

American writer Washington Irving, touring Indian Territory in the 1830s, wrote that the waters of the Arkansas River "look exactly like crayfish soup." Those waters are considerably clearer now. The year 1971 saw the completion of the McClellan-Kerr Arkansas River Navigation System. This mammoth lock-and-dam project opened the Arkansas River and cities as far west as Tulsa to oceangoing vessels. River channels were widened and riverbanks stabilized to prevent erosion. Several lakes in the system were dammed to generate hydroelectric power and control flooding.

FRONTIER LAKES

Oklahoma is called "America's Frontier Lake State." With more than a hundred natural lakes and more than two hundred artificial lakes, Oklahoma has 2,000 more miles (3,219 more kilometers) of shoreline than the country's Atlantic coast and Gulf of Mexico coast combined. Many of these beautiful, clear lakes are state recreation and resort areas and fish and wildlife refuges.

Lake Eufaula, in east-central Oklahoma, is the largest lake in the state. It is a popular vacation spot for boaters, campers, fishing

Grand Lake O' the Cherokees is one of the state's most popular recreation areas.

enthusiasts, and nature lovers. Other lush recreation sites are Grand Lake O' the Cherokees in the northeast and Lake Texoma on the Red River in the south. Tenkiller Ferry Lake, Robert S. Kerr Lake, and Fort Gibson Lake are only a few of Oklahoma's other "frontier lakes."

FLORA AND FAUNA

"Nowhere have I ever seen so many deer, moose, bear and turkey tracks," reported Washington Irving on his Oklahoma tour. Other creatures that make tracks in the state are elk, antelope, rabbits, coyotes, armadillos, horned lizards, and opossums. One of the largest buffalo herds in the world roams in the Wichita Mountains Wildlife Refuge near Lawton. This refuge also has Texas longhorn cattle and a prairie-dog town.

Almost every type of bird between the Rocky Mountains and the Mississippi River can be seen in Oklahoma. These include warblers, sparrows, orioles, cardinals, killdeers, and red-winged blackbirds. Roadrunners abound, but the scissor-tailed flycatcher is the state bird. Once hunted for its long tail feathers, the bird is now protected by a state law.

13

Redbuds, especially lovely during the spring (right), are among the many kinds of trees that are found in Oklahoma.

The Fort Cobb Recreation Area northwest of Anadarko boasts the world's largest crow roost. Tourists gather there in late October to watch as many as 10 million crows descend upon the area. A thicket of elms outside of Shawnee is the roosting spot for hundreds of cattle egrets, herons, and cowbirds.

An amazing variety of trees and grasses are native to Oklahoma. More than 130 kinds of trees are found there, from pine, cedar, and cypress to maple, pecan, blackjack (scrub oak), and redbud. The prairies are ablaze with yellow sagebrush, prairie coneflowers, black-eyed Susans, and butterfly weed. Mesquite, cactus, and buffalo grasses cover the plains.

CLIMATE

In Oklahoma, according to the state song, "the wind comes sweepin' down the plain." Indeed, warm and cold air masses collide over the state and bring drastic temperature changes, high winds, and violent storms. In general, however, the climate is temperate. The north tends to be cooler than the rest of the state, with the east and the south more humid, and the west, dry.

A rainstorm darkens the sky over an Oklahoma wheat field.

The average temperature in July is 83 degrees Fahrenheit (28 degrees Celsius), and January averages 39 degrees Fahrenheit (4 degrees Celsius). Alva, Altus, and Poteau all set Oklahoma's record for the highest temperature in the summer of 1936, at 120 degrees Fahrenheit (49 degrees Celsius). Two towns suffered Oklahoma's coldest recorded temperature of minus 27 degrees Fahrenheit (minus 33 degrees Celsius): Vinita in 1905, and Watts in 1930.

In a year, Oklahoma City averages 32 inches (81 centimeters) of precipitation (rain, snow, and other moisture). The southeast receives about 50 inches (127 centimeters), while the Panhandle averages only 15 inches (38 centimeters) per year.

Tornadoes rip through the state every spring and summer. These violent storms destroy property, injure people, and sometimes take lives. At the National Severe Storms Laboratory in Norman, meteorologists hunt down tornadoes across the nation and measure their barometric pressure and wind speed. They hope to learn how to predict, and perhaps control, these terrible storms.

Chapter 3
THE PEOPLE

THE PEOPLE

Who are Oklahomans? Towns with names like Okmulgee, Nowata, and Tahlequah suggest cultures as old as the state's earliest residents. Names such as Bushyhead, Hog Shooter, and Bowlegs tell of a rough-and-ready frontier people—good-humored, self-reliant, and ready to get down to business. And a down-home sense of contentment is revealed in names such as Goodnight, Cookietown, and Joy. A look at Oklahoma's pattern of growth tells much about its people.

SURVEYING THE RANGE

No other state in the Union was planned as methodically as Oklahoma. After Oklahoma lands became part of the United States, they were settled primarily by decree and design. In 1834, an area including much of eastern Oklahoma was established as Indian Territory. It was here that the federal government resettled thousands of Indians from numerous tribes and cultures. Over the years, but primarily after the Civil War, whites wanted to settle these lands. Before the Oklahoma Territory was formally established in 1890, and in preparation for the first of the land runs, the federal government sent survey teams to the region.

The surveyors' task was to divide up this rough and rangy land into 6-mile (9.6 kilometer) squares. First, the surveyors chose a spot 1 mile (1.6 kilometers) south of Fort Arbuckle as the official

This stone post in Cimarron County marks the point at which the borders of three states come together—Oklahoma, New Mexico, and Colorado.

Initial Point and marked it with a stone column. Through this point they surveyed the Indian Meridian, a line running north to Kansas and south to Texas. Then the surveyors laid out more than seventy north-south "range lines" between Arkansas and Texas. Each range line was parallel to the Indian Meridian; the range lines were 6 miles (9.6 kilometers) apart from one another.

Next, the surveyors mapped out an east-west line running across the state and through the Initial Point. Parallel to the line through the Initial Point, nearly forty lines were drawn every 6 miles (9.6 kilometers) throughout the territory.

Each resulting square was called a township. The surveyors then divided each township into 144 equal squares of land, each about 160 acres (65 hectares). The surveyors marked each corner of these parcels of land with a stone.

Using the stone markers as guides, 50,000 homesteaders in the great Land Run of 1889 tore out across the territory to stake their claims. During the 1893 land run, the population of the state increased by 100,000. More land runs followed, and soon the population of the future state of Oklahoma was spread out nearly evenly across the land.

A CENTURY OF MOVEMENT

When Oklahoma became a state in 1907, it had a population of 1,500,000. According to the 1980 census, its population had doubled to 3,025,495. Where people live in the state has changed, too. Now, two-thirds of all Oklahomans live in urban areas. The capital, Oklahoma City, has the largest population of the state's urban areas. Tulsa is second. Half of all the people in the state today live in the Oklahoma City and Tulsa metropolitan areas. Other major metropolitan areas include Lawton, Norman, and Enid. Nevertheless, the even pattern of Oklahoma's rural roads and farms still reflects those property lines from the old days. Traveling through areas of gridlike farms and ranges can call up visions of the homesteaders' mad dash for the carefully marked-off land.

THE FACES OF OKLAHOMA

Even though less than 1 percent of the population of Oklahoma is foreign-born, the state is a meeting ground of many cultures, races, and ethnic heritages. A look at the people who make up Oklahoma today tells much about the state's history.

Nearly 6 percent of the state's population can claim an American Indian heritage. Some are Indians whose ancestors were there during prehistoric times; others belong to groups that were forcibly moved in from the eastern United States.

Some of the Cherokee, Chickasaw, Creek, and Seminole people brought black slaves with them when they came to Indian Territory. Other blacks moved into the state after the Civil War or laid claims during the land runs. Today, blacks comprise nearly 7 percent of the state's population.

Miners and ranch hands were among the early settlers in Oklahoma. Mining is still an important occupation (left), and descendants of miners who came from Czechoslovakia hold annual festivals (above). The state's "cowboy" heritage is celebrated in statewide rodeos (top).

Many natives of the state are descendants of the soldiers, missionaries, and French and American fur traders who pioneered this new western land after the Louisiana Purchase of 1803.

The mining boom in the Choctaw Nation in the 1870s brought miners from Czechoslovakia, Poland, Russia, Italy, Greece, Scotland, and Wales. Descendants of these miners celebrate their ethnic heritage in colorful annual festivals.

A "cowboy culture" permeates the state, with rodeos in the big cities and many small towns, too. Many Oklahomans are

THE BOSTON AVENUE CHURCH
UNITED METHODIST

Oklahoma's first schools were established by the Five Civilized Tribes. Today, children between the ages of six and seventeen are required to attend school.

The majority of Oklahomans who belong to churches are Southern Baptists or Methodists. The Boston Avenue Methodist Church in Tulsa (left) was the first cathedral-sized church to be built in the Art Deco style of architecture.

descendants of the ranchers and ranch hands of the old cattle-trail days. These were the men who drove great herds of cattle north from Texas, along Oklahoma's famous cattle trails, to the Kansas railway towns.

Some Oklahomans' forebears were the railroad-building crews of the nineteenth century. Others were the Boomers, the Sooners, and the hordes of eager homesteaders of the great land runs. While some of these homesteaders were from other states, the land rush brought people from China, Japan, Mexico, England, France, and Canada as well. The productive wheat farms of the northwest brought German Mennonites and Czechs to the state.

Oklahomans' religious beliefs are rooted in the Southern Baptist and United Methodist denominations. These Protestant denominations support a conservatism that has made Oklahoma a part of the Bible Belt. Other churches, including Disciples of Christ, Presbyterian, Episcopalian, Roman Catholic, and Greek Orthodox, are also represented. The Jewish population is concentrated in the larger urban areas.

OKLAHOMA'S INDIANS

About one-third of the United States citizens of American Indian ancestry live in Oklahoma. There are more Native Americans in Oklahoma than in any other state except California.

When Francisco Vásquez de Coronado first entered the Oklahoma area in 1541, several native peoples were living there. The Kiowa, Comanche, and Plains Apache lived by hunting in the western part of the state. Often these groups were referred to as Plains Indians, as if they were a single group. In the eastern portion of the state, the people were primarily village dwellers and included the Caddo, Wichita, and Pawnee. The Quapaw and Osage also made Oklahoma lands their home.

After the Civil War, the Plains Indians were moved or confined to the western part of the state to make way for the resettlement of five eastern tribes—the Cherokee, Chickasaw, Choctaw, Creek, and Seminole. When they resettled, each of these groups set up a system of government including a constitution, law-enforcement methods, courts, and educational systems. Whites called the tribes the "Five Civilized Tribes." It was these Indians who brought to Oklahoma its first organized system of government.

During the time between the 1803 Louisiana Purchase and statehood in 1907, more than sixty Native American tribes were moved from their ancestral homelands to Oklahoma lands. Sixty-seven tribes representing a variety of cultures and languages now live in Oklahoma.

Today, members of the Five Civilized Tribes comprise more than half the Indian population of the state. Each of these tribes maintains its own form of government within Oklahoma. A nation might publish its own newspaper, engage in commercial ventures, and maintain its own museums and craft centers.

Oklahoma Indians engage in a variety of enterprises. This produce stand in Bixby, just south of Tulsa, is stocked with fruit and vegetables from one of the state's most productive agricultural areas.

The Cherokee Nation has its capital at Tahlequah. The Cherokee Heritage Center there includes a museum and an authentic ancient Cherokee village. The Chickasaw Nation headquarters is in Ada. Chickasaws also own a 627-acre (254-hectare) resort near Allen, with a thunderbird-shaped, five-hundred-seat convention center. Choctaw national headquarters is located in downtown Durant. The Choctaws publish their own newspaper and are involved in many civic and social projects. A large, mound-shaped building marks the Creek National Tribal Complex near Okmulgee. The Creeks' huge Agribusiness Complex includes a commercial dairy farm, large grain plantings, and a beef-cattle project. The capital of the Seminole Nation in Oklahoma is Wewoka. Tribal offices are south of Seminole, on the Mukusukey Mission grounds.

Other Native American groups important in Oklahoma are the Wyandotte, Seneca, Kickapoo, Sac and Fox, and Potawatomie from the northern and eastern United States, and Plains Indians such as the Cheyenne, Arapaho, Kiowa, Comanche, and Apache.

The heritage of Oklahoma's Plains Indians is kept
alive at Indian City, USA, where seven Indian
villages have been re-created (left) and dancers
perform throughout the year (above).
Tsa La Gi Ancient Village in Tahlequah (below) is
an authentic re-creation of a seventeenth-century
Cherokee village.

POLITICAL OKLAHOMANS

Oklahoma has been a one-party state for most of its history. Every Oklahoma governor before 1962 was a Democrat. Most of the senators and representatives Oklahoma has sent to the United States Congress have been Democrats, too. Since the 1970s, however, Oklahomans have lent their support to Republican presidential and congressional candidates.

Several Oklahoma politicians have achieved national fame. Senator Robert S. Kerr, Congressman Carl Albert, and Ambassador Jeane Kirkpatrick are among the most prominent.

Kerr was governor of Oklahoma from 1943 to 1947, and then served in the United States Senate from 1948 until his death in 1963. Called the "uncrowned king of the Senate," Kerr was a powerful leader who served as chairman of the Senate Rivers and Harbors Subcommittee. While in this post, he obtained federal funds for Oklahoma's vast navigation project, the McClellan-Kerr Arkansas River Navigation System.

Carl Albert, an attorney from McAlester, was elected to the United States House of Representatives in 1946. For several years he served as House majority leader. Then he was made Speaker of the House of Representatives, a post he held until he retired in 1976. As Speaker, Albert held the third-highest position in the federal government, after president and vice-president. This is the highest government position an Oklahoman has held.

Jeane Jordan Kirkpatrick was a professor of political science at Georgetown University when President Ronald Reagan named her United States Ambassador to the United Nations. During her 1981-85 term as ambassador, she was frequently outspoken on her views of United States foreign policy. Kirkpatrick has authored *Political Woman* and *The New Presidential Elite*.

Chapter 4
THE BEGINNING

THE BEGINNING

Oklahoma's first settlers arrived nearly twenty thousand years ago, near the end of an era called the Ice Age. They found a land that was much flatter than it is today, with a milder and wetter climate. During that time, a great glacier saddled much of the earth from the North Pole to the northern United States and caused heavy rainfalls. The resulting swamps, savannas, and waterholes of the Oklahoma region provided a perfect environment for Columbian mammoths, giant bisons, and small camels and horses.

THE FIRST OKLAHOMANS

The ancient pioneers made homes on rock ledges and in caves. They were nomadic hunters and roamed the wetlands, prairies, and plains of central and western Oklahoma. Wielding hand-hewn weapons, they hunted the abundant game for food and hides.

Three types of early peoples inhabited Oklahoma. The earliest was Clovis Man, who hunted big game more than fifteen thousand years ago. Next was Plainview Man, living ten thousand years ago. Folsom Man, who occupied Oklahoma eight thousand years ago, was the most recent of these Ice Age peoples. To determine these dates, archaeologists have analyzed flint weapon points and other prehistoric materials found in central and western Oklahoma.

These cliff carvings survive from the time when early Oklahoma people lived in caves and on ledges in the Panhandle's Cimarron Canyon.

As the great glacier melted, Oklahoma's climate, animals, and plants gradually changed. Deer, antelope, and bison, as well as the trees and grasses common in Oklahoma today, began to thrive in the region. The people of this period, called Paleo People, tended to live and move in groups. In spring and summer, they camped on riverbanks, hunted wild animals, and gathered berries, nuts, and seeds. Caves and ledges were their winter homes; during this time, they lived on food they had stored.

Caves in the Panhandle's Cimarron Canyon, near Kenton, reveal much about the Paleo People's life-style. Red painted figures adorn the walls, and carved lines mark the cliffs. Animal bones, cakes made of seeds and berries, corncobs, bone fishhooks, animal-skin bags, and colorful mats and baskets are among the artifacts that have been found in the caves.

Artifacts found in the Spiro Mounds (right) show clearly the highly advanced culture of the Mound Builders.

THE MOUND BUILDERS

Gradually, people settled in the lowlands and valleys of Oklahoma and began to form communites. About 500 B.C., the age of the Mound Builders began. Across the state, people built mounds as house platforms, religious temples, and burial vaults.

About A.D. 800, the Mound Builders' civilization began to flourish in eastern Oklahoma. The Spiro Mounds near Poteau reveal a highly advanced culture that was at its peak between A.D. 1200 and 1350. Artifacts in these burial mounds include engraved conch-shell bowls, copper plaques, textiles, exquisite pottery, sculpture, and ceremonial religious items.

Spiro's prehistoric Indians carried on extensive trade and communication with Indians in Arkansas, Georgia, Alabama, and even Mexico. Their religious rites, particularly, appear to have been influenced by those of Mexico. While most of the Spiro Mound Builders were farmers, others were religious and political leaders, construction workers, and craft specialists.

The inscription on the Heavener Runestone (above), in the Heavener Runestone State Park (left), is believed to have been carved by Norsemen in the year A.D. 1012.

ANCIENT RUNESTONES

Although Spanish explorers are credited with "discovering" Oklahoma in 1541, it is possible that Norse explorers arrived from Greenland more than five hundred years earlier. The evidence is carved in a massive stone on Poteau Mountain in Heavener. Called the Heavener Runestone, it is a huge block of sandstone 12 feet (3.65 meters) high, 10 feet (3 meters) wide, and 16 inches (40.6 centimeters) thick. A strange, eight-character inscription is cut deeply into the stone.

Though scholars continue to study the stone and debate its authenticity, the characters—called runes—are believed to have been carved by Norsemen in the eleventh century A.D. Experts believe the runes represent the date of November 11, in the year 1012. Two other runic inscriptions, found in nearby Poteau and Shawnee, are thought to be the dates November 11, 1017, and November 24, 1024. Similar stones have been found in other areas of the United States.

31

In the year 1541, Spanish explorer Coronado traveled north from Mexico and crossed Oklahoma's eastern Panhandle in search of legendary riches.

Ancient Norse sagas, or legends, tell of four Norse ships sailing across the Atlantic. The Norsemen hoped to set up a colony on the New England coast in 1008. The sagas tell the fates of three of the ships, but nothing is said about the fourth. Some scholars believe the fourth ship may have sailed south around Florida, into the Gulf of Mexico, and up the Mississippi River to the Arkansas and Poteau rivers. Then, as they explored the land near these rivers, the Norsemen could have left their marks in stone.

SPANISH EXPLORATIONS

The arrival of Spanish explorers in 1541 marks the beginning of Oklahoma's recorded history. That year, Francisco Vásquez de Coronado traveled north from Mexico with a small group of Spanish explorers and crossed Oklahoma's eastern Panhandle in search of legendary riches. Although he did not find riches,

Coronado did claim the western half of the Mississippi River Valley—including Oklahoma—for Spain.

In the same year that Coronado was exploring the Southwest, another Spaniard, Hernando De Soto, was exploring the lower Mississippi River Valley. He, too, sought riches. De Soto explored what is now eastern Oklahoma. He claimed all of the lower Mississippi Valley for Spain before he died, in 1542, near what is now Little Rock, Arkansas.

During his expedition, De Soto encountered Chickasaw, Creek, and Choctaw Indians and introduced them to guns and horses. He and some of his men spent time with a community of Chickasaws and took native wives, starting a strain of mixed-blood people.

Other Spanish explorers followed. One of the more notable was Juan de Oñate. In 1601, Oñate set out from Santa Fe in New Mexico, passed western Oklahoma's Antelope Hills, and continued north to what is now the Kansas-Oklahoma border.

FRENCH EXPLORATIONS

Soon French explorers arrived in the area. In 1673, Louis Jolliet and Father Jacques Marquette traveled by canoe from Lake Michigan down the Mississippi River. They traveled along the Mississippi as far as the mouth of the Arkansas River, a few hundred miles from Oklahoma. In 1682, René-Robert Cavelier, Sieur de La Salle, led an expedition all the way down the Mississippi River to the Gulf of Mexico. He claimed the land drained by the western tributaries of the Mississippi River for France. This vast territory he named Louisiana, in honor of the French monarch, Louis XIV. The territory included what is now Oklahoma and much of the same region that had been claimed by Coronado for Spain more than one hundred years earlier.

Fur traders bartered for hides in Oklahoma lands as well as other areas of the country.

New Orleans, founded in 1718 at the mouth of the Mississippi River, quickly became a major trade center for the entire river valley. The first Frenchman to see Oklahoma was a trader named Juchereau de St. Denis. Hoping to set up trade with the Indians, he sailed up the Red River in 1714.

In 1719, Claude du Tisne explored Wichita Indian villages near the Arkansas River. That same year, Bernard de la Harpe left New Orleans to explore the Indian settlements along the Canadian and Arkansas rivers. The daily journals he kept of his wanderings reveal much about Indian life at the time. He wrote that the Wichita and Caddo Indians he met had rich fields of corn, pumpkins, and tobacco, and that they raised fine horses. Every

October, these people left their homes to hunt buffalo in western Oklahoma; they returned in March to plant their fields.

La Harpe had written that Oklahoma's land was fertile and its forests rich with fur-bearing animals. He also claimed the area for France, planting a post bearing the king's coat of arms near Haskell. Now numerous French traders hunted and trapped in Oklahoma lands and traveled Oklahoma waters—the Red, Arkansas, Canadian, Grand, and Verdigris rivers—to bring their goods to market at New Orleans. They set up trading posts and towns and they took Indian wives.

At this time, both Spain and France claimed Oklahoma. Although the Spanish were the first to lay claim to the lands, it was the French who established trade routes, villages, and towns. In efforts to drive them out, the Spaniards regularly invaded the territory. In 1759, Diego Parilla and three hundred Spanish soldiers marched across the Red River and attacked the French settlements of San Bernardo and San Teodoro, called the Twin Villages. With the help of Wichita and Caddo Indians, the French managed to drive the Spaniards off.

Nevertheless, in a treaty of 1762, France ceded the province of Louisiana to Spain. Oklahoma remained under Spanish rule until 1800, when a second treaty returned Louisiana—including Oklahoma—to France.

France paid little attention to its newly regained territory. Napoleon Bonaparte, emperor of France, was occupied with wars of conquest in Europe. American president Thomas Jefferson, however, was eager to expand America's boundaries and open up the western frontier to American settlers. American and French officials met in 1803 and negotiated the sale of the Louisiana Territory to the United States for $15 million. Oklahoma had finally come under the American flag.

Chapter 5
FRONTIER TIMES

FRONTIER TIMES

The land that is now Oklahoma has gone by many names. In 1803, the Louisiana Purchase lands were called the District of Louisiana. Congress put this district under the jurisdiction of William Henry Harrison, the Indiana territorial governor at that time. In 1805, Congress named this vast area Louisiana Territory. After 1812, when the state of Louisiana entered the Union, the rest of the territory west of the Mississippi River was renamed Missouri Territory. As the state of Missouri prepared to enter the Union in 1819, what is now Arkansas and most of Oklahoma became the Territory of Arkansaw (later changed to "Arkansas").

In 1825, Congress declared most of present-day eastern Oklahoma to be Indian Territory. In 1890, the western portion of Indian Territory was named Oklahoma Territory. Together, the two were sometimes called the Twin Territories. The Panhandle, annexed in 1890, was called everything from No Man's Land to Robber's Roost. By statehood in 1907, Americans had taken the rest of Indian Territory from the Indians. The new state of Oklahoma then extended east to the Arkansas border.

During these frequent name changes, four groups of people moved into this new American land. Settlers came to make new homes and to hunt, trap, and trade. Explorers came to study and map the new territory. Soldiers arrived to protect the new frontier. Finally, Indians from other regions came to make new homes in the territory—most of them against their will.

Among the explorers sent by President Thomas Jefferson to map the Louisiana Territory was Zebulon Pike, whose party reached what is now Oklahoma's eastern border.

EXPLORERS

At the time of the Louisiana Purchase, it was not clear where, exactly, Louisiana's boundaries were. Spain held that its southern boundary was the Arkansas River, in north-central Oklahoma, while the United States held that the Red River to the south was the true boundary. President Thomas Jefferson sent out army exploring parties to map the area in hopes of settling the dispute.

Captain Richard Sparks set out in 1806 with orders to follow the Red River north and west to its source. When he reached the southeastern corner of Oklahoma, however, a force of Spanish soldiers turned him back. That same year, Captain Zebulon Pike was sent to explore the Arkansas River. Pike's party started from St. Louis, Missouri and crossed Missouri and Kansas to meet the Arkansas River. Pike then split up his party. While Pike himself continued westward toward the Rocky Mountains, he ordered Lieutenant James Wilkinson to continue down the Arkansas River. As winter came, and the river began to freeze, some members of Wilkinson's party found themselves tossed into icy waters and dodging great chunks of drifting ice. On New Year's Day, 1807, the Wilkinson party finally reached Belle Point, on Oklahoma's eastern border.

George C. Sibley's expedition in 1811 took him through the Great Salt Plains of north-central Oklahoma. He described the plains as "glistening like a brilliant field of snow in the summer sun." Sibley rightly predicted that these salt deposits would someday have great commercial value.

In 1817, Major Stephen Long was sent to establish a fort on the Arkansas River. He chose Belle Point, which became Fort Smith, Arkansas. In 1819, Long was ordered to find the source of the Arkansas River and that of the Red River as well. He was to follow them back to American settlements in Oklahoma. Long found the source of the Arkansas in the Rocky Mountains. He ordered a party led by Captain John R. Bell to follow it all the way back to Fort Smith. Long himself found and followed what he thought to be a branch of the Red River. Later, he realized he had followed the Canadian River, a tributary of the Arkansas. So he, too, arrived in Fort Smith, only four days after Captain Bell.

Thomas Nuttall's 1819 expedition into Oklahoma was a scientific venture. A famous naturalist, Nuttall collected valuable information about eastern Oklahoma's plants, animals, rocks, and minerals. His *Journal of Travels in the Arkansas Territory* is one of the first scientific records of Oklahoma's wildlife and geology.

SOLDIERS AND FORTS

While some soldiers were sent out to explore Oklahoma, others were assigned to establish forts. The soldiers were to protect the settlers against invading Spaniards who still disputed the

The stockades of Fort Gibson, built in 1824, have been reconstructed.

territory's southern border. In addition, they were to protect the Indians who came to settle in eastern Oklahoma from the Plains Indians to the west.

In addition to Fort Smith, on the Oklahoma-Arkansas border, soldiers built Fort Gibson in the northeast and Fort Towson in the southeast in 1824. Forts Washita, Arbuckle, and Cobb were completed by 1860. Towns grew up around the forts, along with stores, churches, roads, and farms. The soldiers helped map the territory, carried mail, and protected the wagon trains bringing new settlers.

The ruins of Fort Gibson, near Muskogee, and Fort Washita, near Durant, are still standing, and their stockades have been rebuilt. Fort Sill, near Lawton, is in operation today as the United States Army's artillery school.

Among the famous military leaders stationed at Oklahoma forts were Zachary Taylor, a hero of the Mexican War and, later, president of the United States; Robert E. Lee, commander of the Confederate forces during the Civil War; and Jefferson Davis, later president of the Confederate States of America.

INDIAN REMOVALS

As the United States grew in the early nineteenth century, the white population sought more land for settlement. Many settlers were attracted to the fertile agricultural lands of the southeastern United States—Georgia, Florida, Alabama, and Mississippi. This territory, however, was the ancestral home of five Indian groups: the Cherokee, the Choctaw, the Creek, the Seminole, and the Chickasaw. Because many of these Indians had adopted the customs of Europeans and white Americans, the whites called them the Five Civilized Tribes.

Some whites ignored the Indians altogether and moved onto their lands; others led brutal raids on Indian villages. Settlers continued to pressure the federal government to remove the Indians from the southeastern lands and open the lands to whites for homesteading. After all, the whites reasoned, frontiersmen in the Ohio River Valley had been pushing Indians west for years.

In 1804, Congress passed the first act allowing the president to order Indians out of their tribal lands to be resettled in western "Unassigned Lands." The area west of Arkansas Territory would later be designated Indian Territory. The federal government acted to relocate all Indians who lived anywhere east of the Mississippi River into this one area.

Some Indians relocated quietly and effectively. The more well-to-do Indians built beautiful homes and established plantations,

Missionaries throughout the young country worked to convert the Indians to Christianity.

which were worked by their black slaves. They brought their goods to the trading posts to sell or barter. In their dress and their customs, they were much like their white neighbors. Missionaries brought Christianity to Indian Territory. Soon many Indian churches and academies were set up. But many more Indians did not wish to move. It was these Indians who were the target of the grueling and bloody process of Indian removal. In 1818 and 1825, federal agents pressured the Osage and Quapaw of northeastern Oklahoma to sign treaties giving up their lands and to move west. This made room for new tribes to be moved in.

With the election of President Andrew Jackson in 1828, the removal of the eastern tribes intensified. In 1830, Congress passed the Indian Removal Act, and with it assigned the president still greater powers over the Indians. More troops were sent to Fort Gibson and Fort Towson in Indian Territory. In 1834, General

The Choctaws, the first of the Five Civilized Tribes to be removed to Indian Territory, were painted by George Catlin as they engaged in a "Ball Play Dance."

Henry Leavenworth and Colonel Henry Dodge led an expedition to persuade the Indians of western Oklahoma to accept and make room for the new tribes that would be arriving. They signed peace treaties with Wichita, Caddo, and Comanche leaders.

The first of the Five Civilized Tribes to be removed to Indian Territory were the Choctaws. In 1820, by the Treaty of Doak's Stand, the Choctaws ceded land in Mississippi to the United States in return for land in southern Oklahoma. By treaties in 1826 and 1832, the Creeks of Alabama and Georgia signed away their lands and agreed to move. Seminoles in Florida and Chickasaws, who were spread over several eastern states, signed removal treaties in 1832. A group of Georgia Cherokees signed in 1835.

Some Georgia Cherokees felt that the representatives who signed the treaty did so without proper authority. They took their case to the Supreme Court. Though the court agreed that the treaty was invalid, the state officials paid no heed and President Jackson did nothing to enforce the court's ruling.

Endless Trail, by artist Jerome Tiger, evokes the sadness, pain, and misery experienced by the Cherokees during their forced march from Georgia to Indian Territory.

THE TRAIL OF TEARS

The final removal of these tribes was a travesty. Fifteen thousand Indians were forced out of their homes and herded into camps to watch as their belongings were looted and their homes were burned to the ground. Government troops drove them without mercy along the long, hard trail west to Indian Territory. Indians lost what little livestock and personal property they had been able to take with them. Starvation, exposure to cold, and disease drastically cut their numbers. The forced march during the bitter winter of 1838-39 is remembered as the worst of them all. Because of these inhuman conditions, this trip came to be known as the Trail of Tears.

The Five Civilized Tribes eventually reestablished their ways of life in Indian Territory. Each nation established its capital, set up a tribal government, established a school system, and elected leaders. They wrote tribal constitutions, although these had to win the approval of the United States government. The federal government assured the Indians that this new land would be theirs "as long as grass shall grow and rivers run."

CIVIL WAR AND RECONSTRUCTION

The onset of the American Civil War in 1861 threw Indian Territory into turmoil. Several southern states had seceded from the Union and formed the Confederate States of America. At once, the Confederates saw Indian Territory as an important "buffer zone" between North and South. Confederate leader Albert Pike was sent to persuade the Indians to fight for the Confederacy. In return, the Confederate government promised that it would protect the Indians' lands when the war was over.

Some Indians decided to fight for the Union side. Others decided not to fight at all. Many of the slaveholding Indians sided with the Confederacy. Others joined the Confederate cause because of unhappiness with the federal government. Several Confederate Indian regiments were formed. Their commanders were leaders from the various Indian nations—Douglas Cooper, Tandy Walker, D.N. McIntosh, Chilly McIntosh, John Jumper Drew, and Stand Watie.

Bloody battles were fought in and around Indian Territory. Cherokee troops under Stand Watie fought bravely, but lost, in the battles of Pea Ridge, Honey Springs, and Locust Grove. Watie was promoted to brigadier general in 1864 and was put in command of most of Oklahoma's Confederate forces.

Watie's troops scored a great victory when they captured a three-hundred-wagon Union supply train in the Battle of Cabin Creek. Nevertheless, Confederate defeats in the eastern United States brought the war to an end. On April 9, 1865, General Robert E. Lee surrendered to General Ulysses S. Grant. One by one, other Confederate leaders surrendered. Of the Confederate officers in Oklahoma, Brigadier General Stand Watie was the last to lay down his arms.

During the Second Trail of Tears, these Plains Indians were forcibly relocated to reservations farther west.

The government's plan for bringing the southern states back into the Union was called Reconstruction. During Reconstruction, the Indian nations of Oklahoma suffered many losses. Their slaves were freed. They were required to permit railroad companies to lay tracks across their land. The Five Civilized Tribes were required to sign the Reconstruction Treaties of 1866. Through these treaties, the government took much of the Indian Territory land that had been assigned to the Five Civilized Tribes and confined them to smaller areas in eastern Oklahoma. The Plains Indians of western Oklahoma—tribes that traditionally roamed and hunted on the Great Plains—were confined to reservations. Plains tribes were forced to settle on reservations in the west, and the Five Civilized Tribes were pushed to the east. Once again, large groups of Indians were forcibly relocated. This movement has been called the Second Trail of Tears.

Chapter 6

A DEVELOPING PERSONALITY

A DEVELOPING PERSONALITY

The time between the end of the Civil War in 1865 and statehood in 1907 was a colorful period in Oklahoma's history. The great cattle drives left trails across the territory. Oklahoma cowboys became local and national folk heroes. Rodeos were a popular entertainment, and Oklahoma's Wild West Shows toured the world. The oil boom made the petroleum industry a major economic base for the future state. And the land runs filled the area with people eager for statehood.

CATTLE TRAILS AND COWBOYS

After the Civil War ended in 1865, many foods were in short supply across the country. Most important for Oklahoma, beef in particular was in short supply in the North and East. In the Great Plains of Texas, however, were vast herds of longhorn cattle. Spaniards had brought the longhorns into Mexico in the 1500s, and the herds had multiplied and spread northward. The longhorns were so plentiful that some ranchers even slaughtered cattle to reduce the beef supply and bring prices up.

Meanwhile, railway lines were spreading west across Kansas, and new towns were springing up along these new trade routes. Famous Kansas towns such as Dodge City, Abilene, and Wichita grew rapidly. They were major centers for shipping railway cargo from the South and the West to the North and the East. Texas

11225

Modern cowboys round up a herd.

ranchers hired cowboys, called cattle drovers, to drive their longhorn herds north from Texas across Oklahoma to the Kansas rail towns. As they crossed Oklahoma, the drovers followed certain established cattle trails.

One of the first trails was the East Shawnee Trail, which ran through the state in a northeasterly direction from the Red River to the Arkansas River and into Missouri. The East Shawnee Trail followed a route known as the Texas Road. Settlers and merchants had used the Texas Road for years in traveling between Texas and Missouri. Today, Highway 69 and the Missouri-Kansas-Texas railroad echo the Texas Road. The West Shawnee Trail branched away from the East Shawnee and headed northwest toward Wichita, Kansas. The most famous trail was the Chisholm Trail, named for Cherokee trader Jesse Chisholm. It took a straight north-south course through west-central Oklahoma and linked

As rail lines began to extend through Oklahoma into Texas in the 1880s, the days of the great cattle drives drew to a close.

Texas and Kansas. Today, the Rock Island railroad and U.S. Highway 81 follow the path of the Chisholm Trail, passing just west of Oklahoma City. The Great Western Trail in the west ended in Dodge City, Kansas. Farther west, the Jones-Plummer Trail crossed the Panhandle.

As more Oklahoma homesteaders began to farm, they also began fencing their land. The fences made uninterrupted cattle drives difficult. Furthermore, as rail lines began to extend through Oklahoma into Texas in the 1880s, there was less need to drive the cattle to the trains. By 1890, the days of the great cattle drives were drawing to a close.

Cowboys who worked on cattle ranches or cattle drives were highly skilled. They had to be able to rope cattle, wrestle them to the ground for branding, and break wild horses to be used for work. Ranch hands sometimes matched their skills against one another, and different ranches would boast that they had the finest cowboys. Eventually, the competitions went public, and the rodeo became a popular spectator sport.

From 1888 to 1913, Pawnee Bill toured the world with his Wild West Show.

WILD WEST SHOWS

The Wild West Show grew out of the cattle-driving days. Rancher Gordon W. Lillie, whose ranch was near Pawnee, became famous as "Pawnee Bill." For a while, Pawnee Bill toured with Buffalo Bill Cody's Wild West Show. Then, from 1888 to 1913, he toured the world with his own Pawnee Bill's Wild West Show. One of the stars was Lillie's wife, May. A refined woman from Philadelphia, May became an excellent markswoman and sidesaddle bronco rider.

Another popular show was organized by George Washington Miller and his three sons on their ranch near Ponca, Oklahoma. Opening in 1907, the Miller Brothers' 101 Ranch Real Wild West Show toured the United States and foreign countries until the Great Depression. Some of its stars were Bill Pickett, the black cowboy who invented steer wrestling; Tom Mix, who starred in many silent cowboy movies; and Lucille Mulhall, the "world's first cowgirl."

Among the stars of the Miller Brothers' 101 Ranch Real Wild West Show were Bill Pickett, the black cowboy who invented steer wrestling (top left), and Tom Mix, who starred in many silent cowboy movies (above). Pawnee Bill (left) was the star of his own Wild West Show.

Miss Mulhall was the daughter of Oklahoma rancher Zack Mulhall, who first featured her in his own Wild West Show. There she amazed audiences—including President Theodore Roosevelt—with her horseback riding, cattle roping, and steer-tying skills.

THE OIL BOOM

Oil has colored Oklahoma's history since territorial days. In 1889, Edward Byrd, a "wildcatter" (oil prospector) from Kansas, drilled Oklahoma's first oil-producing well near Chelsea. Then in 1897, Frank Phillips drilled the state's first commercial oil well in Bartlesville. Twenty years later, in 1917, he founded the Phillips Petroleum Company in Bartlesville, and in 1928 opened the first Phillips service station. The oil boom was on as drillers discovered more rich deposits of the liquid they called "black gold."

Oil, or petroleum, is millions of years old. It is derived from prehistoric plants and animals that lived on the earth about half a billion years ago. Organic matter from those plants and animals was broken down over time until it became the energy-rich liquid we use today. Powerful drills cut deep into the earth's surface to reach the oil, buried by tons of rock and soil.

Drillers, sometimes called "mud hogs," came upon the Red Fork oil field near Tulsa in 1901. The nearby Glenn Pool was found in 1905. Before long, Tulsa was dubbed the Oil Capital of the World. When Henry Ford built his Model T in 1908, the age of the automobile began. The new demand for fuel meant big business for Oklahoma's mud hogs.

Oil "boom towns" soon covered the state: Bartlesville, Ponca City, Ardmore, Seminole, Tonkawa, Cushing, Avant, Okmulgee, and many others. One of the most important boom towns was Oklahoma City. Born the day of the Land Run of 1889, this city sits atop one of the richest oil fields in the world. When drillers first struck oil there in 1928, the well gushed out 6,500 barrels of oil every twenty-four hours.

One well on the Oklahoma City field captured the nation's fancy. When the drill struck on March 26, 1930, "Wild Mary

Towering oil derricks can be seen in nearly every Oklahoma county. When drillers struck oil at the site of "Wild Mary Sudick" (inset) in 1930, the well spewed black crude oil for eleven days before it could be capped.

Sudick" spewed black crude oil high above the 100-foot (30-meter) rigs. For eleven straight days Wild Mary Sudick gushed. The well yielded 20,000 barrels a day and splattered homes and livestock for miles around. Because natural gas was released with the oil, people in the area were forbidden to strike matches until the crisis was over.

Newsman Floyd Gibbons gave reports on Mary's condition twice a day. The stories were translated and broadcast on radios around the world. Finally, on April 6, 1930, a "death-defying crew" of engineers was able to cap Mary with a specially made "bonnet" to control the flow. The name of the man who supervised the effort was H.M. Myracle.

BOOMERS AND SOONERS

In the 1870s, the central part of Indian Territory was known as the Unassigned Lands. These lands had not been assigned to any particular Indian tribe by the Reconstruction treaties of 1866. The region soon took on the aura of a "promised land." Railway companies, farm-equipment manufacturers, wholesalers, and financial institutions—as well as single families and homesteaders—decided they had the right to stake claims there.

Many companies hired professional promoters, called Boomers, to organize and lead homesteaders into the Unassigned Lands. Once homesteaders had occupied the land, companies would enter the territory and open up businesses.

The most successful of the Boomer leaders was Captain David L. Payne. A frontier scout, Union army soldier, and Kansas Territory legislator, Payne was a forceful and disciplined leader. Payne arrived in southern Kansas in 1879. He quickly mustered Oklahoma-bound homesteaders into neat, orderly "Boomer camps" along the border. Payne led Boomer groups into Oklahoma several times. One group got as far as the North Canadian River in central Oklahoma. There the settlers built a stockade and a town and began preparing fields for planting. Soon, however, troops from nearby Fort Reno uprooted the homesteaders and escorted them out of the Unassigned Lands back to the Kansas border.

Eventually, the federal government was so pressured by business and private groups that it agreed to open the Unassigned Lands for settlement. In March 1889, President Benjamin Harrison announced that at noon on April 22, the 2 million acres (.8 million hectares) of Unassigned Lands would no longer be leased to the Indians. The lands would be opened to white settlers.

Fifty thousand land-hungry home seekers stampeded across the Oklahoma border at noon on April 22, as the Land Run of 1889 began.

As the date of the Oklahoma "land run" drew near, land-hungry home seekers converged along the Kansas and Arkansas borders. Nervous tensions, sometimes erupting into pistol-wielding violence, filled the air. There was not enough land to go around. Some settlers tried to sneak into the territory sooner than the official starting time. It was those "Sooners" who gave the state its nickname, the Sooner State. Federal troops caught many of the Sooners and marched them back to the border. Others got away with their ploy. They staked their claims and then, just before the law-abiding land runners arrived, ran their horses to near-exhaustion to make it appear as if they had just arrived.

Finally, at noon on the appointed day, the official pistol shot rang out and the Land Run of 1889 began. Fifty thousand people stampeded across the borders. Entire towns appeared where there had been empty plains before. Oklahoma City was founded in a day, becoming a tent city of ten thousand occupants. Guthrie acquired a population of fifteen thousand overnight.

MORE LAND RUNS

In May 1890, Congress passed the Oklahoma Organic Act. This act declared the western half of Indian Territory to be Oklahoma Terrritory. The Oklahoma Organic Act also established a territorial government and provided for a territorial governor, a supreme court, and a two-house legislature. This marked the beginning of Oklahoma's progress toward statehood. Oklahoma's state government today is based on the same territorial government system set up by the 1890 Organic Act.

Guthrie was named the territorial capital, and President Harrison appointed George W. Steele as the first territorial governor. In August 1890, the voters in Oklahoma Territory went to the polls and elected delegates to the legislature. When the assembly convened later that summer, the delegates spent much of their time arguing over a new site for the capital.

The Oklahoma Organic Act also stated that any Indian lands that would be opened for settlement in the future would become part of Oklahoma Territory. The Panhandle, or "No Man's Land,"was also annexed to Oklahoma Territory, thus opening it for settlement.

Other land openings followed, as government officials bargained with Indian leaders for rights to their lands. President Harrison appointed the Dawes Commission in 1887 to work with the Five Civilized Tribes in the east and the Jerome Commission in 1900 to negotiate with the western Plains Indians. The commissioners offered to an Indian leader an allotment of about 160 acres (65 hectares) of land per member of his tribe. The amount of the allotment varied according to the fertility of the land and which tribe was to hold it. The commission then subtracted that amount of land acreage from the total land that had been originally assigned to the tribe. The government then declared that the remaining land was "surplus land" and purchased it. This changed the Indians' type of land ownership from tribal ownership to what was called allotment in severalty. The change meant, effectively, that the amount of land available to the Indians was severely reduced. Furthermore, the concept of individual ownership was contrary, in many cases, to the Indians' social and community ethic.

Lone Wolf, a Kiowa leader, appealed the formation of the Jerome Commission to the Supreme Court. In his case, he charged that the changes in land ownership violated the terms of earlier treaties the government had made with the Kiowa. The appeal was denied; the Supreme Court declared that Congress had the right to do away with the provisions of an Indian treaty.

As each new chunk of Indian land was opened to white settlement, it was added to Oklahoma Territory. The 1891 land run included areas that had belonged to the Iowa, Sac and Fox, Shawnee, and Potawatomi Indians. Cheyenne and Arapaho lands, now west-central Oklahoma, were opened in 1892. In 1893 came the great run for the 6-million-acre (2.4-million-hectare) Cherokee Outlet in the northwest. The Kickapoo run took place in 1895.

Greer County, in the southwest corner of the territory, was annexed in 1896 after the United States Supreme Court ruled that Texas's claim to it was invalid. Wichita, Caddo, Comanche, Kiowa, and Apache lands were opened to settlement by lottery, instead of by land run, in 1901. Finally, the so-called Big Pasture lands along the Red River in the south were opened in 1906—for sale to the highest bidder.

Piece by piece, the Oklahoma Territory had spread itself out until it reached the borders that are Oklahoma's today. The next step for this rough-and-tumble territory would be statehood.

Chapter 7
INTO THE
TWENTIETH CENTURY

INTO THE TWENTIETH CENTURY

On September 17, 1907, Oklahoma voters went to the polls. They approved the state constitution that had been drawn up earlier that year by their constitutional convention. They also elected Democrat Charles N. Haskell as the state's first governor.

The approved state constitution was forwarded to Washington, D.C. There the United States Congress voted to approve it, and on November 16, 1907, President Theodore Roosevelt signed Oklahoma's official statehood proclamation. Oklahoma became the forty-sixth state of the Union. The news was telegraphed to the capital at Guthrie, and crowds awaiting the proclamation burst into cheers.

Shortly thereafter, the Oklahoma legislature met for the first time. Many of the progressive measures voted into law at that first session are still in force. Safety codes were adopted for mines, and laws were passed to protect children from being forced to work. The legislature passed factory-inspection laws and workmen's compensation measures for job-related injuries.

At that time, much of the country was concerned that large companies might become powerful enough to set prices as high as they wished. To guard against such a monopoly occurring in the railroad industry, the legislature set a ceiling on railway fares. Governor Haskell was especially concerned about banks. To prevent bank "runs" and bank failures, he took special measures to stabilize financial institutions. A number of public-education

The inauguration of Charles N. Haskell, Oklahoma's first governor

laws were passed. Teachers were required to be certified, and
children between the ages of eight and sixteen were required to
attend school. The state constitution also prohibited the sale of
liquor. This law remained in effect until 1959.

The legislature enacted a series of "Jim Crow" laws. These
required that black people use "separate but equal" facilities for
transportation, education, and other public services. It was not
until the 1950s that United States Supreme Court decisions
outlawed these segregation practices.

Governor Haskell, a Democrat, hoped to move the state capital
away from Guthrie, which was a Republican stronghold. On
June 11, 1910, Oklahomans were asked to vote on the location of
the state capital. The choices were Guthrie, Oklahoma City, and
Shawnee. Although the vote did eventually favor Oklahoma City,

Governor Haskell's secretary removed the state seal from Guthrie before the count was official. Shocked citizens in Guthrie protested, saying that the state capital had been stolen, but there was nothing they could do. The state was governed from the rented Lee-Huckins Hotel in Oklahoma City until a state capitol building was completed in 1917.

When it achieved statehood, Oklahoma's economy relied mainly on farming and fuel production. In the second decade of the 1900s, prices for these products were low, which hurt the state's economy. When the United States entered World War I, however, Oklahomans prospered once again with the increased demand for food and fuel products.

THE TROUBLESOME TWENTIES

When the war ended in 1918, the demand for food and fuel dropped, the prices for these goods dropped, and again the state's economy suffered. In the early 1920s, Oklahomans endured massive unemployment, business collapses, and failures of farms, ranches, and oil-producing industries throughout the state. Workers staged strikes and riots. Many of them were agitated by socialists, who demanded that the people have more control over the economy. More trouble was stirred up by members of the militant antiblack society known as the Ku Klux Klan, who attempted to blame the blacks for the economy's woes.

Governor James Robertson, who served from 1919 to 1923, faced many difficulties. He used the National Guard to quell labor riots, took measures to curb the Ku Klux Klan, and dealt with brutal race riots that broke out in Tulsa. In the midst of these problems, 1,300 miles (2,092 kilometers) of paved highways were built during his term.

IMPEACHMENT FEVER

Oklahoma's constitution had provided for a strong legislature. The members of the constitutional convention had hoped to prevent any Oklahoma governor from having too much power. As a result, the state legislature could rather easily impeach a governor (charge him with misconduct). After a trial, the governor could be removed from office. Governor Lee Cruce missed being impeached in 1912 by one vote. Governor James Robertson escaped impeachment in 1921, also by one vote.

Governor John C. Walton, who took office in 1923, served the shortest term of any Oklahoma governor—only ten months. Walton had run on an anti-Ku Klux Klan platform and dissidents banded together to impeach him. He endangered Oklahoma's state budget by approving lavish expenditures of state monies. To appease warring political factions, he awarded political jobs to members of all sides. He forced board members of Oklahoma's state colleges to resign and appointed his own people to the college boards. Both students and citizens protested this move. Finally, the state legislature brought twenty-two formal charges against Walton and voted to remove him from office. Walton's successor, Lieutenant Governor Martin Trapp, was welcomed as a conservative. Among other things, Trapp repealed $10 million worth of Walton's expenditures.

Governor Henry S. Johnston, elected in 1927, was impeached in 1929. Although Johnston did not abuse his power as Walton had, the state legislature had opposed him from the start. His support of Democratic presidential candidate Al Smith offended state politicians who favored Republican Herbert Hoover. The charges brought against Johnston were flimsy. Nevertheless, the legislature removed him from office.

During the Dust Bowl years of the 1930s, thousands of Oklahomans packed up their belongings and left the state.

THE DUST BOWL YEARS

Oklahoma suffered terribly during the 1930s. The stock market crash of 1929 had ushered in the Great Depression. The demand for fuels dropped. Then, in the 1930s, a severe drought in the Great Plains transformed much of the southwest United States, including Oklahoma, into what was known as the Dust Bowl. Crops failed, and high winds swept the arid topsoil into blinding dust storms. For many Oklahomans, already reeling from the economic setbacks of the 1920s, this was a grim and desperate time. Thousands of Oklahoma farmers, miners, and oil workers packed up their families and their belongings and left the state. Author John Steinbeck chronicled this period in his novel *The Grapes of Wrath*.

During much of this time, the state was led by William H. "Alfalfa Bill" Murray, who served as governor from 1931 to 1935. Murray was a colorful, frontier-style character, and a strong political leader. He forcefully attacked the pressing problems of unemployment and business failures. He even donated much of his salary to feed the needy. When he and the state legislature

Wagoner County (above) suffered from the combined effects of the Great Depression of the 1930s and the devastating Dust Bowl years that followed. Posters of the time advertised government help for farmers who had lost their land to dust storms.

clashed, Murray stood firm. On one occasion he announced to them, "... if you've got any impeachment ideas in your heads, hop to it. It'll be like a bunch of jackrabbits tryin' to get a wildcat out of a hole."

DAWN OF PROSPERITY

World War II brought new prosperity to Oklahoma. Governor Robert S. Kerr, the first governor to be born in Oklahoma, led the state in its war efforts. Manufacturers, miners, oil producers, farmers, and ranchers all worked diligently to produce war

Tinker Air Force Base in Midwest City (above) played an important role in World War II. After the war, construction of Oklahoma's first turnpike began, and more highway construction followed. Scenic Talimena Skyline Drive (left), built in the 1960s, winds through Talimena State Park in the Ouachita National Forest.

supplies and materials. Oklahoma's military facilities, such as Fort Sill in Lawton and Tinker Field in Midwest City, saw intense activity. Governor Kerr also improved Oklahoma's colleges and eliminated the state's $37 million debt.

Many Oklahomans had left the state in the 1930s because of the depression and the Dust Bowl. But by the mid-1950s, the population had recovered. Oklahoma's economy blossomed, with many new construction projects and new industries taking hold. The state began to rely less on agriculture and more on industry.

Construction of Oklahoma's first turnpike began in 1949 during Governor Roy Turner's term. When it was completed in 1953, the Turner Turnpike connected Oklahoma City and Tulsa. The 1950s saw more highway construction. Congress created the interstate highway system in 1956, giving Oklahoma its Interstates 35, 40, and 44. The roads were a sign of the state's recovering economy.

In 1954, the United States Supreme Court ruled that it was unconstitutional for a state to maintain separate schools for white and black students. Governor Raymond Gary, who served from 1955 to 1959, spent much of his term arranging for the peaceful desegregation of Oklahoma's public schools.

Senator Robert Kerr, a former Oklahoma governor, worked to get federal funding for the massive Arkansas River navigation project. Under construction from 1947 to 1970, this project provided many jobs for Oklahomans. It also gave the state a good source of hydroelectric power and an ultramodern shipping route. With the completion of the McClellan-Kerr Arkansas River Navigation Project, goods in cities as far inland as Tulsa could reach the Gulf of Mexico via water. These features made the state an attractive location for new businesses.

Oklahoma's industries continued to grow in the 1960s and 1970s. Oklahoma City became an important aviation center, with Tinker Air Force Base and the Federal Aviation Agency Aeronautical Center located there.

Manufacturing activities in Oklahoma have grown tremendously in recent decades, with plants tending to locate in or near Oklahoma City and Tulsa. Oklahoma is now an important producer of electronics equipment, aviation and aerospace craft, automobiles, computers, and many other products in high demand today.

Throughout the 1970s, petroleum and natural-gas industries were Oklahoma's major source of income and employment. When oil prices dropped in the early 1980s, the state's focus shifted to other sectors of the economy. Now Oklahomans are relying more on manufacturing and other industries. Meanwhile, they look forward to a gradual revival in the state's traditional economic strength, the production of fossil fuels.

Chapter 8
GOVERNMENT AND THE ECONOMY

GOVERNMENT AND THE ECONOMY

GOVERNMENT

Oklahoma, like the United States, is ruled by three branches of government. The executive branch is composed of the governor and other top state officials; the legislative branch includes the 48-member state senate and the 101-member state house of representatives; the judicial branch consists of judges who interpret the law.

Oklahoma's state constitution was approved by the state's citizens and by the federal government in 1907. Those who framed the constitution wished to limit the powers of the governor and to give the citizens a strong role in making the laws. Oklahoma's state government today reflects those wishes.

Until 1970, the governor, or chief executive, was limited to two four-year terms. After that year, a governor could serve more than two terms, though no more than two consecutive terms. The governor appoints the secretary of state, the budget and revenue chiefs, and several state commissioners. Other executive officials, such as the attorney general, superintendent of public instruction, and lieutenant governor, are elected by the people.

The main lawmaking body is the state legislature, which meets in the capital of Oklahoma. Like the United States Congress, it consists of a senate and a house of representatives. Senators are elected to four-year terms. Senatorial elections are held every two years to assure smooth changes in the makeup of the senate. Representatives serve two-year terms.

While the legislature makes most of the laws, the citizens of Oklahoma may also take a direct role in lawmaking. Through a process called initiative and referendum, voters may either propose a law or pass a law by popular vote.

Nine judges preside over Oklahoma's supreme court. They hear appeals of decisions made in lower civil courts. The supreme court may assign some of its cases to a six-member court of appeals. The court of criminal appeals hears cases appealed from lower criminal courts. A nominating commission proposes judges for the higher courts, and the governor makes the final selection. After judges serve for one year, they must run for election by the voters to a six-year term. District and county judges are elected to four-year terms.

Each of Oklahoma's seventy-seven counties is run by three commissioners. A city council with a mayor or a council manager governs most cities and towns.

Grants from the federal government provide about one-fourth of the state's income. Much of the rest comes from individual and corporate income taxes, sales taxes, motor-fuel taxes, and oil-and gas-production taxes. Taxes on items such as tobacco, insurance, and alcoholic beverages also provide revenue for the state.

EDUCATION

Oklahoma's first schools were established by Native Americans and modeled after the best schools in the East. The Cherokees were the most advanced educators. They had their own alphabet and writing system, invented in 1821 by Cherokee leader Sequoyah.

In 1907, Oklahoma's first state legislature created a state board

These ninth-grade students attend Sequoyah High School in Tahlequah, named in honor of the man who invented the Cherokee alphabet.

of education and instituted free public schools and compulsory attendance. Now, children between the ages of six and seventeen are required to attend school. Oklahoma has more than a thousand public elementary schools, more than eight hundred public middle and secondary schools, and more than eighty private elementary and secondary schools.

The governor appoints members of the state board of education; the superintendent of public instruction is elected by the people. Three boarding schools for Native American students are maintained by the federal government.

Oklahoma established a teacher-training college in 1890 — Oklahoma Normal School (now Central State University) in Edmond. In 1892, two more institutions of higher learning were established — the University of Oklahoma in Norman and Oklahoma Agricultural and Mechanical College (now Oklahoma State University) in Stillwater. These universities — along with Bacone College, established in 1880 — are the oldest of Oklahoma's twenty-two accredited colleges and universities.

The University of Oklahoma's Bizzell Library is the Southwest's second-largest library. Included among its special research collections are extensive western-history archives and collections on business history and science history. The university's Medical

Coal ranks third, after oil and natural gas, among Oklahoma's leading mineral products.

Center, in Oklahoma City, includes colleges of medicine, dentistry, nursing, and other health-related professions.

THE ECONOMY

Oklahoma's major industries are manufacturing, social and government services, wholesale and retail trade, and mining. Manufacturing accounts for about 20 percent of the state's gross output. Goods manufactured from raw materials in Oklahoma include industrial machinery, electronics and metal equipment, and rubber, plastic, and glass goods. Oklahomans holding government service jobs include those at Fort Sill in Lawton and Tinker Air Force Base near Oklahoma City.

Fuel production and mining activities are spread throughout the state and account for 11 percent of the state's gross product. Towering oil rigs and bobbing oil pumps can be seen in nearly every county in the state.

Ottawa County in northeastern Oklahoma belongs to the Tri-State District. At one time, this was the richest lead- and zinc-producing region in the world. Rich coal deposits were discovered in Pittsburg County in the Choctaw Nation in the 1870s.

Salt is mined in the north-central Great Salt Plains region. Gypsum is found in the Gypsum Hills area of western Oklahoma. The state's other mining resources include limestone, red granite, sand, gravel, and clays. Oklahoma is also the leading state in the production of helium gas.

Lumbering is important in eastern Oklahoma, where there are forests of pine as well as hardwoods such as oak, hickory, ash, and walnut. Sawmills produce pulpwood and fiberboard as well as lumber for construction and furniture making.

OIL FLUCTUATIONS

Since the discovery of rich oil and natural gas deposits in Oklahoma in the late 1800s, the energy industry has played a major role in the state's economy. Steadily rising oil prices throughout the 1970s brought a wealth of new businesses and workers into the state. In the prosperous 1981-82 period, the oil and gas industries accounted for nearly 24 percent of Oklahoma's gross state product.

In 1982 and again in 1986, the price of oil dropped worldwide. The drop drastically affected America's oil-producing states. Oklahoma—as well as Texas, Louisiana, and New Mexico—suffered the loss of income, jobs, and businesses. Unemployment in Oklahoma reached an all-time high of 9.2 percent in 1986. In 1987, oil and gas revenues had dropped to 11 percent of the state's gross output.

The situation is steadily improving, however. Oil prices appear to be steady or rising. Oklahomans are also developing other sectors of their economy. The state's economic forecasters are cautious, but predict that Oklahoma will see a slow, steady recovery over the coming years.

Beef production is Oklahoma's major agricultural activity, and wheat is the state's leading cash crop.

AGRICULTURE

Agriculture accounts for about 3 percent of Oklahoma's gross state product. Beef production is the major agricultural activity. While herds of grazing beef cattle are a reminder of the old cattle-trail days, today the use of modern feedlots to fatten cattle is more common. Oklahoma City's livestock market is one of the largest in the Southwest.

In the 1940s, cotton, corn, and wheat were the state's major crops. Today, wheat is the state's leading cash crop as well as its most important export crop. Together, beef and wheat account for 70 percent of Oklahoma's agricultural income. Hay is a major money crop, as are peanuts, soybeans, corn, cotton, and sorghum.

77

Interstate 44, running through Tulsa (right) and Oklahoma City, connects with expressways in neighboring states to provide a continuous divided highway from Chicago, Illinois to Wichita Falls, Texas.

TRANSPORTATION

From the days of the European explorers through the times of the fur traders and cattle drovers, transportation has been of central importance to Oklahoma. In the past few decades, the state has been crisscrossed by superhighways, toll roads, and interstate highways. Many of these roads parallel trails first established by traders or Indians. Interstate 44, running northeast to southwest, includes the Will Rogers Turnpike, the Turner Turnpike, and the H. E. Bailey Turnpike. It connects with expressways in neighboring states to provide a continuous divided-highway route from Chicago, Illinois to Wichita Falls, Texas. Oklahoma's other turnpikes are the Indian Nation, Cimarron, and Muskogee.

Interstate 35 is a direct north-south route that passes through Oklahoma City. Interstate 40 cuts through the center of the state from east to west. It was once part of the legendary Route 66, stretching all the way from the Atlantic to the Pacific Ocean.

About 80 percent of Oklahoma's roads are paved. Railroad lines cover about 5,600 miles (9,000 kilometers). Before the railroads,

A barge being loaded on the McClellan-Kerr Arkansas River Navigation System, Oklahoma's major commercial waterway

steamboats traveled up the Mississippi River to dock as far north as Fort Gibson on the Neosho River near Muskogee.

The McClellan-Kerr Arkansas River Navigation System is Oklahoma's major commercial waterway. Opened in 1971, the waterway is 445 miles (716 kilometers) long. The lock-and-dam channel extends from the Mississippi River through Arkansas and into northeastern Oklahoma. The system of locks and dams allows commercial barges to transport minerals, grains, chemicals, paper, steel, and petroleum products from Oklahoma to the Gulf of Mexico and then to worldwide commercial ports. In its first year of operation, the waterway carried 4.3 million tons (3.9 million metric tons) of cargo.

Oklahoma's major commercial airports are in Oklahoma City and Tulsa. There are about 130 other public airports throughout the state. Fourteen of the nation's major airlines make stops in Oklahoma. The national headquarters of the Federal Aviation Administration (FAA) is in Oklahoma City. All federal air traffic controllers in the country are trained there. Oklahoma's interest in flight is not confined to the earth. Several of the nation's astronauts are native Oklahomans, including Owen K. Garriott, Thomas P. Stafford, and Gordon Cooper.

Chapter 9
CULTURE AND RECREATION

CULTURE AND RECREATION

Oklahoma, said historian Angie Debo, is "more than just a state. . . . Here all the American traits have been intensified. The one who can interpret Oklahoma can grasp the meaning of America in the modern world."

It has been said that people tell the most about themselves by the things they make and the ways they play. If that is so, then Oklahomans' arts and leisure activities reveal who they are in a unique way.

ARCHITECTURE

Styles of architecture in Oklahoma vary widely and include soaring towers, Victorian mansions, and earthen mounds. The prairie-style influence of architect Frank Lloyd Wright is seen in many of Oklahoma's office complexes and public buildings. In the 1920s, he built the impressive Richard Lloyd Jones home in Tulsa. Later, in 1955, Wright designed Bartlesville's Price Tower, a combination office and residential building.

Oil barons and other wealthy Oklahomans of the early 1900s built European-style mansions. Waite Phillips's Italian Renaissance villa in Tulsa has become the Philbrook Art Center. Oklahoma City's elegant Overholser Mansion is a picture-book Victorian residence.

The state capitol building and the Oklahoma Historical Society building feature the Greek Revival style. Oklahoma's state capitol

This ultramodern structure is the prayer tower at Oral Roberts University in Tulsa.

is one of only seven state capitols that does not have a dome. The Creek Nation Tribal Complex just outside of Okmulgee presents a sharp contrast to the typical office building. The large, circular mound-shaped building houses tribal business offices.

In Oklahoma City is the award-winning Stage Center at Festival Plaza near Myriad Gardens. Featuring a modern, high-tech style, it is part of Oklahoma City's Central City Redevelopment Area. Another ultramodern structure is the prayer tower at Oral Roberts University in Tulsa.

PERFORMING ARTS

Five world-famous ballerinas have come from Oklahoma; all claim a Native American heritage. Maria Tallchief has been the prima ballerina of the New York City Ballet and founded the Chicago City Ballet. Her sister, Marjorie Tallchief, danced with the Paris Ballet Company. Yvonne Chouteau, at fourteen, was once the youngest member of the Ballet Russe de Monte Carlo. Moscelyne Larkin, also of the Ballet Russe, became co-director of the Tulsa Civic Ballet. Rozella Hightower opened a ballet school in Cannes, France.

Summer and autumn powwows feature Native American dance and spectacular exhibitions and contests.

For Native American dance, summer and autumn powwows and the August American Indian Exposition in Anadarko feature spectacular exhibitions and contests.

Many cities and towns support local symphony orchestras. Among them are the Oklahoma City Symphony, the Tulsa Philharmonic, and the Lawton Symphony. Young musicians from all over the world come to play in the Tri-State Music Festival. The festival, sponsored by Phillips University, is held in Enid. Music clinics and private instruction for young people are conducted throughout the state. The University of Oklahoma, Oklahoma State University, and other institutions have excellent music departments.

ARTS AND CRAFTS

Many fine artists came out of Dr. Oscar Jacobson's School of Indian Art at the University of Oklahoma. Starting in the 1920s, he encouraged his students to use their memories of tribal themes,

Creek-Seminole artist Jerome Tiger, whose career had barely begun when he died in 1967 at the age of twenty-six, used pencil and white tempera to depict the Five Civilized Tribes.

customs, and ceremonies. This tradition continues to guide Oklahoma Indian artists. It can be seen, for example, in the stylistic, hauntingly simple paintings of Acee Blue Eagle, the emotionally charged paintings and sculptures of Jerome Tiger, and the sensitive wood sculptures of Willard Stone. Today, Bacone College students and graduates are world renowned for their works in traditional Indian styles as well as realistic and non-objective styles.

Charles Banks Wilson is another of the state's well-known artists. In the state capitol rotunda are his life-sized portraits of famous Oklahomans such as Sequoyah and Jim Thorpe, and murals of Oklahoma's history. The late Augusta Metcalf, who grew up on the frontier, painted highly detailed scenes of frontier life. John Noble, who participated in the land run of 1893, is best known for his painting *The Run*.

Native American craftspeople today produce beautiful beadwork, featherwork, silver jewelry, suede items, dolls, shawls, and many other products.

The Philbrook Art Center in Tulsa was the gift of oilman Waite Phillips.

MUSEUMS

Many of Oklahoma's museums display art and artifacts pertaining to the state's frontier history. Oklahoma's largest museum is the National Cowboy Hall of Fame and Western Heritage Center in Oklahoma City. It includes the National Rodeo Hall of Fame and the Great Western Performers Hall of Fame. Also in Oklahoma City is the state's oldest museum, at the Oklahoma Historical Society.

Indoor and outdoor exhibits and demonstrations highlight the Museum of the Great Plains in Lawton. An outdoor sculpture garden along tree-lined walkways is the setting for Anadarko's National Hall of Fame for Famous American Indians.

Muskogee's Five Civilized Tribes Museum features sculptures and paintings by modern-day tribe members. The Southern Plains Indian Museum in Anadarko includes an outlet for the Oklahoma Indian Arts and Crafts Cooperative. Multimedia exhibits present the Cherokee story from prehistoric times to the present at the Cherokee National Museum in Tahlequah. Nearby is the Tsa-La-Gi Ancient Village. This is an authentic re-creation of a seventeenth-century Cherokee settlement.

Several museums are gifts from wealthy Oklahomans. The Thomas Gilcrease Institute of American History and Art in Tulsa contains the collections of its founder, oilman Thomas Gilcrease. Oilman Frank Phillips founded the Woolaroc Museum near Bartlesville. It features a Chinese jade collection, a large Indian blanket collection, and works by southwestern artists Frederic Remington and Charles Russell. Tulsa's Philbrook Art Center is in oilman Waite Phillips's Renaissance villa, surrounded by beautifully landscaped grounds.

LITERATURE

Since territorial days, Oklahoma has produced fine writers, most notably poets John Rollin Ridge, a Cherokee, and Alexander Posey, a Creek.

Will Rogers, a humorist of Cherokee descent, was known and loved around the world through his humorous newspaper columns. Songwriter Woody Guthrie touched many hearts with his musical tales of hard times. Lynn Riggs's play *Green Grow the Lilacs* was the basis for the spectacularly successful Rodgers and Hammerstein musical *Oklahoma!* A 1969 Pulitzer Prize in fiction went to Kiowa novelist N. Scott Momaday for *House Made of Dawn.* Oklahoma City-born Ralph Ellison, a teacher and lecturer on black culture, is best known for his 1952 novel *Invisible Man.*

Historian Angie Debo, who died in 1988 at the age of ninety-eight, came to Oklahoma by covered wagon. She rose to national prominence as a historian and received many honors and awards. Among her thirteen books are *Oklahoma, Foot-Loose and Fancy-Free,* and *The Rise and Fall of the Choctaw Nation.* The Public Broadcasting System featured a one-hour documentary on Angie Debo's life and works in its series "The American Experience."

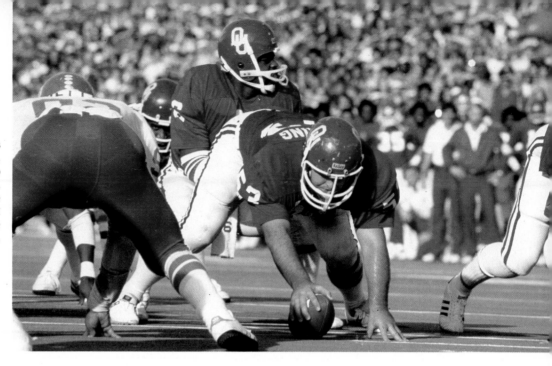

College football is popular in Oklahoma, especially when two Oklahoma teams compete. In this game, the University of Oklahoma battled Oklahoma State University.

SPORTS AND ATHLETICS

Many native Oklahomans have achieved national and international acclaim through sports and athletics.

Jim Thorpe, part Sac and Fox and part Potawatomi, has been called the world's greatest athlete. Born near Prague in 1887, he won the pentathlon and the decathlon in the 1912 Olympics in Stockholm, Sweden.

Other world-class athletes from Oklahoma include gymnast Bart Connors, an Olympic gold-medal winner, and wrestler John Smith, the 1987 world champion.

Although the state does not have a professional baseball team, Oklahomans have often followed the World Series with family pride. Warren Spahn, Mickey Mantle, and Johnny Bench are among the dozens of favorite sons who have played for winning World Series teams. Hall-of-Famer Mantle credited milking sixteen cows a day and wielding a sledge hammer in the mine for his remarkable hitting power!

Oklahomans are equally proud of the University of Oklahoma football team, the Sooners. They have won more games in the last fifteen years than any other college football team. The team, led by coach Barry Switzer, ranked number one in college football's Division I-A as they went into the 1988 Orange Bowl game. In number of national championships, the Sooners rank second only to Notre Dame. And the Sooners have won eighteen of the twenty-six major college bowl games they have entered.

"If you're going to lose, you might as well lose by fifty, right?" Opponents of the University of Oklahoma's Sooner basketball team often adopt this attitude. Known for their speed, the Sooners averaged 103.5 points per game in the 1987-88 season. Goaded by coach Billy Tubbs to "remember where nice guys finish," the Sooners racked up scores in the 130s, 140s, and even 150s. They reached the National College Athletic Association (NCAA) Final Four and beat Arizona in the semifinals.

OUTDOOR RECREATION

Vacationers enjoy motor boating, waterskiing, and fishing on Oklahoma's many lakes and rivers. The state has more than two hundred artificially created lakes, more than any other state. Some of the most popular lakes are Lake Eufaula, Grand Lake O' the Cherokees. Lake Texoma, Fort Gibson Lake, Tenkiller Ferry Lake, and Keystone Lake. Oklahoma is proud to rank third in the nation in its amount of fishable fresh water.

Along five of Oklahoma's lake sites are lavish state resorts with golf courses, tennis courts, hotels, cottages, and restaurants. Lake Texoma Resort is the most popular. Others are Lake Murray Resort, Western Hills Guest Ranch, Quartz Mountain Resort, Fountainhead, Arrowhead, and Roman Nose Resort.

Most of Oklahoma's state parks are alongside lakes. The state has thirty-two state parks and twenty-eight state recreation areas. There are also forty-eight state wildlife management areas throughout the state's waterways, forests, hills, and prairies. For nature lovers, there are dozens of official hiking and backpacking trails, canoe trails, and equestrian trails.

HORSING AROUND

Horses have been vital to Oklahoma's history and economy since its earliest days. With a horse population of about 500,000, Oklahoma claims more horses per capita and more horses per square mile than any other state. Horse-related activities bring over $1 billion a year into the state's economy.

Annual horse shows include the World Championship Quarter Horse Show, the World Championship Appaloosa Show, and the National Miniature Horse Show and Convention.

There are rodeo competitions throughout the state. A typical rodeo features some standard events: calf roping, bull riding, steer wrestling (also called bulldogging), bareback bronc riding, and saddle bronc riding.

The finals of the International Professional Rodeo Association are held in Tulsa every January. Several hundred other rodeo competitions are held throughout the state every year. Guthrie hosts the Women's National Finals Rodeo and the Ben Johnson Pro Celebrity Roping and Cutting Rodeo. Pawnee holds the Pawnee Bill Memorial Rodeo.

Other equestrian entertainments include polo matches and horse-farm tours. Eight of the state parks feature stables with rental horses. Some parks offer guided trail rides, hayrides, stagecoach rides, and moonlight rides.

Annual horse shows in Oklahoma include the World Championship Quarter Horse Show, the World Championship Appaloosa Show, and the National Miniature Horse Show and Convention.

Pari-mutuel horse racing is an exciting attraction at Blue Ribbon Downs near Sallisaw. Crowds can see some of America's fastest quarter horses, Thoroughbreds, Appaloosas, Paints, and Arabians compete on its oval track and straightaway. Racing enthusiasts can also enjoy the lavish Remington Park horse-racing complex in Oklahoma City.

FESTIVAL FEVER

Oklahomans love to celebrate. Festivals and contests throughout the state celebrate Oklahoma's frontier glories, ethnic roots, and even favorite plants and animals.

Dozens of towns hold rodeos and Indian powwows. An Indian powwow is a festival of song, dance, special ceremonies, and other activities. The powwow is one way Native Americans may renew and solidify their sense of oneness as a people. Oklahoma's annual powwows are the Potawatomi in Shawnee, the Sac and Fox in Stroud, the Cheyenne in Clinton, the Comanche in Walters, and the Quapaw and the Pawnee in towns of the same name. The Tulsa Powwow is a large intertribal gathering.

91

Two of the most popular Oklahoma events are the Muskogee Azalea Festival (above) and the Stilwell Strawberry Festival (right).

Visitors to an Indian powwow may be treated to some of the state's traditional Indian foods. Some of the more unusual include blue dumplings or corn biscuits, which contain bean or pea ashes, and shuck bread, made with corn shucks. Possum-grape dumplings, poke salad, and singed squirrel are delightful dishes, each with its own secrets.

Guthrie, the territorial capital, hosts the annual Eighty-Niner Celebration in honor of the great Land Run of 1889. Muskogee features an Azalea Festival, and an annual Strawberry Festival takes place in Stilwell.

The annual Kolache Festival in Prague, a Czech town of about 2,400 people, draws as many as 35,000 visitors. This and the Czech Festival in Yukon feature folk dances and lavish outlays of ethnic foods. There is also an Italian Festival in McAlester, a Hispanic Festival in Tulsa, and Octoberfests in several cities.

Entrants in the Rattlesnake Derby in Waurika earn a "certificate of bravery" for competing in a snake hunt. Spectators, meanwhile, may feast on snake steaks. The Shortgrass Rattlesnake Derby in Mangum offers prizes for the longest, shortest, and heaviest captives.

Oklahomans who love to fish may enter one of the many fishing contests held throughout the state, or they may choose to cast their lines in the waters of Lake Murray (left) or another of the state's "frontier lakes."

For Oklahomans who love to fish, there are a number of fishing contests. Some of them are the Walleye Rodeo in Canton, the Crappietown Tournament at Lake Eufaula, and bass tournaments in Purcell, Sulphur, Muskogee, and Arnett.

Other contests and celebrations are unique to the state. Broken Arrow has held its annual Rooster Day Celebration since 1930. Festivities honoring the rooster include a parade and the crowning of Miss Chick. Gage honors a bird of a different feather in its Roadrunner Marathon and Festival. Gate features Bone Pickin' Day, while Langley holds an annual Noodling Contest. Weatherford claims the World Championship Watermelon Seed Spitting Contest. For heroic displays of frontier skills, the Brick and Rolling Pin Throwing Contest in Stroud rivals the National Cow Chip Throwing Contest in Beaver.

From classical dance to cow-chip throwing, Oklahomans have kept a variety of traditions alive and are proud to share them with visitors to the state.

Chapter 10

A TOUR

A TOUR

Oklahoma has been called the "Land of Six Countries." Its terrain ranges from rugged peaks to grassy prairies and verdant woods. Woven into the landscape is its history—the story of the people who built a civilization out of this land.

FRONTIER COUNTRY

In the heart of Frontier Country lies the state's capital, Oklahoma City. On the day of the Land Run of 1889, it sprang up overnight as a tent city of ten thousand people. Today, with a population of more than four hundred thousand, it is a city of glistening white state buildings, glass-and-concrete office complexes, modern shopping districts, medical centers, and convention and entertainment centers. Yet the frontier days, and the frontier spirit, live on.

Oklahoma City's central business district, only a fifteen-minute drive from Will Rogers World airport, has been rejuvenated. The Central City Redevelopment Area boasts the ultramodern Myriad Convention Center—a sports, entertainment, and convention facility. At Festival Plaza nearby is Stage Center, an award-winning example of innovative modern architecture.

An exciting part of the city is completely underground. Beneath the central business district is the Metro Concourse—twelve blocks of underground tunnels lined with shops and restaurants.

Crowds gather at the Festival of the Arts in Oklahoma City.

In the northeast section of the city is Oklahoma City's State Capitol Complex. The capitol itself sits atop an oil field that was productive until the 1980s. Inside the capitol rotunda is a fascinating display of the state's art and history. Here murals and portraits by artist Charles Banks Wilson honor famous Oklahomans and tell the state's history in vivid, dramatic scenes.

A short distance from the capitol is the Oklahoma Heritage Center, a frontier-era mansion with parlors and formal gardens. Nearby is the Heritage Hills Historic Area, which preserves homes built by Oklahoma's nineteenth-century founders. One of these is the elegant Overholser Mansion, built by entrepreneur Henry Overholser. This Victorian mansion contains the owner's original furnishings. The third floor ballroom is now a costume gallery displaying clothing from the 1870s through the 1970s.

Nearby is the Oklahoma City Zoo. Many rare animals are kept here, including the golden lion marmoset and the Indian rhino.

The nearby Kirkpatrick Center includes the sprawling Omniplex, the largest science and technology museum in the Southwest. The center also houses the Photography Hall of Fame, the Oklahoma Aviation and Space Hall of Fame, and the Indian American Center. At the Kirkpatrick Planetarium, daily sky shows present the mysteries of astronomy and mythology.

Not far away is the National Cowboy Hall of Fame and Western Heritage Center. Owned and operated by seventeen western states, the center houses actor John Wayne's impressive collection of guns, knives, saddles, art works, and priceless Indian kachina dolls. Other exhibits portray the life of the early settlers and honor pioneers, western movie stars, and rodeo heroes.

Heading north from Oklahoma City, one travels through beautiful, rolling hills into a piece of living history. This is Guthrie, the capital of Oklahoma Territory and, between 1907 and 1910, the state capital.

A walk through Guthrie's fourteen-block historic district reveals one hundred historic buildings. This is the largest array of Victorian commercial buildings in the world. An Eastern European architectural style, with Romanesque arches and onion-shaped domes, adds flavor to many of these buildings.

Eighty-Niner Week is Guthrie's annual celebration of the great Land Run of 1889. Guthrie was one of the many towns that grew up overnight in April of that year.

A short drive to the northeast leads to Horsethief Canyon. Here legendary outlaws such as Bill Doolin and the Dalton Gang hid from pursuing lawmen. From the high bluffs overlooking the Cimarron River, one can easily imagine those horsemen dashing furiously around the bends far below.

The buffalo herd at the Wichita Mountains Wildlife Refuge near Lawton numbers more than six hundred.

GREAT PLAINS COUNTRY

Southwest of Oklahoma City is the Great Plains region. The landscape rises in gentle, rolling swells, peaking in the Wichita Mountains. Here is Anadarko, a great center of Indian culture and arts. At the Southern Plains Indian Museum and Crafts Center, beautiful silver and leather craftwork are on display. Items by Comanche, Apache, Pawnee, Kiowa, Caddo, Mohawk, Sac and Fox, and other Indian craftspeople are sold in the gift shop.

The nearby National Hall of Fame for Famous American Indians is a sculpture garden spread out along a rolling landscape. Memorialized here in bronze busts are Indian explorers, artists, thinkers, and warriors. The twenty-six bronzes, on pedestals, are placed along a gracefully shaded walkway.

A short distance south of Anadarko, in the Tonkawa Mountains, is Indian City, USA. The highlight of Indian City, USA is the guided tour of seven ancient Indian villages. These villages have been planned and constructed by the University of

Oklahoma Anthropology Department. Every detail of the dwellings, furnishings, clothing, and everyday utensils is authentic. As the tour winds through the forest, an Indian guide tells fascinating anecdotes. Along the route are an Apache wickiup, a Caddo lodge, a Wichita village, a Kiowa camp, a Pawnee lodge, a Navajo hogan, and a Pueblo adobe. The American Indian Exposition held here every August is a spectacular festival of war-dance contests, pageants, and greyhound and horse races.

Not far from Anadarko is the Wichita Mountains Wildlife Refuge, near Lawton. At the entrance, a stark warning sign greets visitors: Open Range—Buffalo and Longhorn Are Dangerous—Keep Your Distance. The road winds through mile after mile of rolling hills and undulating prairielands.

Visitors may see herds of longhorn cattle, but the timid buffalo may be harder to find. Once numbering some 60 million, buffalo were the largest population of land animals ever to exist. By the late 1800s, however, they were almost extinct. Conservationists and government agencies have begun to rebuild herds. Fifteen buffalo were brought to the Wichitas in 1907 and, with careful management, the herd has grown to about 625.

Rocky Mountain elk and native deer are also protected here. The rugged, rocky outcroppings, oak forests, and grassy prairies are an excellent habitat for the refuge's four-legged residents. Amid a glistening sea of golden prairie flowers, there is even a prairie-dog town.

A few miles to the southeast lies Lawton's Fort Sill Military Reservation. The museum complex here is a national historic landmark. The nineteenth-century buildings form a western heritage museum. Apache chief Geronimo and several other Indian chiefs are buried on Fort Sill's grounds.

This llama knows how to keep cool on a hot summer day in the Arbuckle Wilderness. Not far south of that scenic area is Lake Murray Resort and State Park (far right), which features a number of recreation facilities.

LAKE COUNTRY

To the east of the Great Plains are the mountains and waterways of Lake Country. The craggy Arbuckle Mountains near Sulphur are very old. Once as massive as the Rocky Mountains, they have eroded into unusual geologic formations.

Nestled in the mountains is the Arbuckle Wilderness, a 400-acre (162-hectare) park with a scenic drive. This is not the usual scenic drive—here, more than two thousand exotic animals from all over the world roam free. Among the many species wandering through the wilderness are llama, yak, gnu, giraffe, lion, ostrich, kangaroo, antelope, and bighorn sheep.

Nearby, the Chickasaw National Recreation Area is full of campsites, boating areas, and nature trails. Seven springs in the area pump out sulphur and bromide water into a network of creeks and streams. The Travertine Nature Center displays live plant and animal specimens from the area, provides information on nature trails, and offers ecology and natural-history programs.

Fort Washita, near Lake Texoma, once provided protection for the Chickasaws against the Plains Indians.

West of the Arbuckle Wilderness is Turner Falls, Oklahoma's largest falls. Its sparkling waters tumble 77 feet (23 meters) down the Arbuckle Mountains into a deep-blue pool.

A short drive to the south, past Ardmore, is Lake Murray Resort and State Park. For rugged nature-lovers, this 115,000-acre (46,539-hectare) park offers many hiking trails and scenic landscapes. There are also lavish facilities for those who want the comforts of civilization in the wilderness. The resort offers a lodge and cottages, a golf course, and a paved airstrip.

A 30-mile (48-kilometer) jaunt to the east is sparkling, blue-green Lake Texoma. This is Oklahoma's most popular resort area. Like Lake Murray, it features a lodge, cottages, recreation facilities, and an airstrip. Fishing enthusiasts catch crappie, bass, catfish, and sunfish.

Clustered around Lake Texoma are some fascinating historical sites. Fort Washita once provided protection for the Chickasaws and Choctaws against the Plains Indians. The Arrowhead Museum in Tishomingo contains such items as Indian stone artifacts and fossils. In the same town is the Chickasaws' original log council house, their first capitol in Indian Territory.

The map shows: Spiro Mounds State Park, Pocola, Heavener, Poteau Mountain, Winding Stair Mountain, Oachita Mountains, Kiamichi Mountain, Oachita National Forest

Talimena Skyline Drive, which winds through the Ouachita Mountains, offers scenic views such as this.

KIAMICHI COUNTRY

The southeastern section of Oklahoma is called Kiamichi
Country, named for the Kiamichi Mountains. State Highway 2
goes through the region from south to north. The road curves
through wooded alpine mountains, blue with distant mist, that
slope down to rich, blue-green valleys.

The most distinctive geographical feature in the southeast is the
mountainous Ouachita National Forest. This rough woodland
covers 1.5 million acres (.6 million hectares) of Arkansas and
southeastern Oklahoma. The mountains and forests attract artists,
nature lovers, and hikers from all over the country.

The Ouachitas are Oklahoma's highest mountain range. The
Talimena Scenic Drive winds through these mountains and hugs
the crest of Winding Stair Mountain. The drive extends from
Talihina, Oklahoma to Mena, Arkansas.

North of the Ouachitas near the Arkansas border is Heavener,
home of the Heavener Runestone. To reach the stone, visitors
must drive up the gentle inclines of Poteau Mountain. At the top
of the mountain, a stone stairway leads down into a little valley

The twelve mounds at Spiro Mounds State Park are remnants of Oklahoma's Mound Builder culture, which flourished from A.D. 850 to 1450, and are the site of the state's only archaeological state park.

where the massive runestone is encased in a glass shelter. Its strange inscription is a haunting memorial of the eleventh-century Norsemen who are believed to have carved it.

About 30 miles (48 kilometers) to the north is Spiro Mounds State Park. This site is Oklahoma's single archaeological state park. The twelve mounds are remnants of Oklahoma's Mound Builder culture, which flourished from A.D. 850 to 1450. A museum in the park displays some of the Mound Builders' artifacts and religious ceremonial items. The University of Oklahoma Archaeology Department supervises the excavations, and visitors may tour selected areas of the grounds.

Just east of Spiro, tucked away on a rural road, is Pocola's Central Glass Company. Here, great sheets of thick glass are sent through furnaces so they can be bent into curved glass for buildings, greenhouses, and cabinets. Occasionally, a visitor may be able to observe a master glassblower blowing graceful glass swans and elegant vases.

**Dewey Bartlett Square,
in the Main Mall of Tulsa**

GREEN COUNTRY

Northeastern Oklahoma is called Green Country. Much of this region lies in the foothills of the Ozark Mountain range.

Tahlequah, the Cherokee national capital, lies in the wooded hills north of Tenkiller Ferry Lake. Street signs in Tahlequah are printed in both Cherokee and English. At the Cherokee Heritage Center amphitheater, the Trail of Tears story is retold through a dramatic presentation every June through August. At Tsa-La-Gi Ancient Village, Cherokees demonstrate the daily tasks, crafts, and skills of their ancestors.

In nearby Muskogee is the Five Civilized Tribes Museum, showing a large collection of modern Indian art. The Thomas-Foreman home in Muskogee reflects the historical and literary interests of Dr. and Mrs. Grant Foreman, authorities on the history of the Five Civilized Tribes and eastern Oklahoma.

Just outside of Muskogee is the Fort Gibson Military Park. Now rebuilt, the original stockade on this outpost was built in 1824. Mexican War hero and United States president Zachary Taylor was once stationed at Fort Gibson, as was Confederate president Jefferson Davis.

Tulsa, Oklahoma's second-largest city, offers many opportunities for recreation and culture. Williams Center, in the heart of downtown Tulsa, is a nine-block development that includes the elegant Performing Arts Center. In the Main Mall, cars are prohibited and pedestrians can enjoy the Bartlett Square Fountain or listen to a noontime concert of live music.

At Swan Lake Park, bird lovers may relax to the sights and sounds of swans, geese, and other wild birds. Not far away are the massive, wrought-iron gates of the Philbrook Art Center, which is housed in an Italian Renaissance villa surrounded by sculptured gardens and lawns. Once the home of oilman Waite Phillips, the museum contains Phillips's collections of Chinese jades and American Indian art and basketry.

Gilcrease Museum, on the northwest side of Tulsa, centers on oilman Thomas Gilcrease's personal collection. The museum has expanded the original collection, which now includes Western art, pre-Columbian artifacts, exciting bronze sculptures by Frederic Remington, and paintings by Charles Russell.

Side trips out of Tulsa should include Claremore and Bartlesville. The Will Rogers Memorial in Claremore features thirteen dioramas by artist Jo Mora, showing scenes from Rogers' life. Also on display are his collection of saddles, mementos from his vaudeville and Hollywood days, letters from famous people, and copies of his films.

In Bartlesville, home of oil magnate Frank Phillips, is the famous Price Tower, designed by architect Frank Lloyd Wright. Just outside of town is the Woolaroc Museum. Situated in a wildlife refuge, this was once Phillips's country lodge. Inside are 55,000 individual exhibits of Western art and artifacts. Outside, roaming the grounds, are buffalo, oriental silka deer, Brahma and Scotch Highland cattle, peacocks, and ostriches.

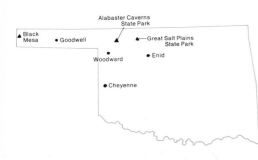

This rock formation near Black Mesa in the Panhandle is called School Marm

RED CARPET COUNTRY

Northwestern Oklahoma, including the Panhandle, is Red Carpet Country. On the Panhandle's western tip looms Black Mesa, the highest point in the state. Also on the Panhandle is No Man's Land Museum in Goodwell. Exhibits tell the story of life in the Panhandle, once known as No Man's Land.

Halfway down the western edge of the state, near Cheyenne, are the Black Kettle Museum and the Washita Battlefield. This is the site of the 1868 Battle of Washita, between General George Custer and Chief Black Kettle's Cheyenne warriors. In the museum are Indian relics and old cavalry items. Some 70 miles (113 kilometers) north of here is Fort Supply. This was Custer's headquarters during his battles against the Plains Indians.

About 30 miles (48 kilometers) north of Woodward is Alabaster Caverns State Park, the largest public gypsum cave in the country. This underground cavern is a wonderland of multicolored alabaster and selenite crystals. Outside, trails lead down to Cedar Canyon, where Indians and outlaws once hunted and camped. One trail arrives at the Natural Bridge, a rock bridge spanning the canyon.

Alabaster Caverns, the largest public gypsum cave in the country, is a wonderland of multicolored alabaster and selenite crystals.

Some 50 miles (80 kilometers) to the east, near Cherokee, is Great Salt Plains State Park. From April through October, the public may dig for selenite crystals in the Great Salt Plains Selenite Crystal Area.

From here, a southerly course toward Oklahoma City leads to the town of Enid. This is the home of Vance Air Force Base, the largest jet-training command in the country. Also in Enid is the Museum of the Cherokee Strip, with artifacts from the area's pioneer settlement days. Here, too, is Phillips University, sponsor of the national Tri-State Music Festival.

A short trip south from Enid brings the tour full circle—back to Oklahoma City.

Only after scaling Oklahoma's craggy peaks, luxuriating along its lakeside nature trails, and gazing in haunting silence across its open plains can a person truly know Oklahoma. For such a visitor, it comes as no surprise that Oklahomans carry in their hearts these words from the state song:

> We know we belong to the land
> And the land we belong to is grand!

OKLAHOMA

FACTS AT A GLANCE

GENERAL INFORMATION

Statehood: November 16, 1907

Origin of Name: A combination of two Choctaw words—*okla*, meaning "people," and *hummus*, meaning "red"; thus, Oklahoma means "red people."

State Capital: Oklahoma City, founded 1889

State Nicknames: Sooner State official state nickname; also called the Boomer State; other nicknames are Land of Six Countries and America's Frontier Lake State

State Flag: An Osage warrior's circular buckskin shield, decorated with seven eagle feathers and with six crosses that symbolize stars, or high endeavor. The shield is crossed in the shape of an X by an olive branch, the white man's symbol of peace, and a calumet, or Indian peace pipe. The background is a field of blue, signifying devotion. The design was adopted on April 2, 1925, and the name Oklahoma was added to the flag in 1941.

State Motto: *Labor Omnia Vincit* ("Labor Conquers All Things")

State Bird: Scissor-tailed flycatcher

State Animal: American buffalo or bison

State Flower: Mistletoe (named the "flower emblem" in 1893)

State Wildflower: Indian blanket

State Tree: Redbud

State Rock: Barite rose rock

State Fish: White bass or sand bass

Before it burned down in 1980, Golda's Old Stone Mill near Stilwell was the only water-powered mill operating in Oklahoma and one of the few remaining grist mills in the country.

State Song: "Oklahoma!" from the musical *Oklahoma!* with words by Oscar Hammerstein II and music by Richard Rodgers:

Brand new state! Brand new state, gonna treat you great!
Gonna give you barley, carrots and pertaters,
Pasture fer the cattle, Spinach and Temayters!
Flowers on the prairie where the June bugs zoom,
Plen'y of air and plen'y of room,
Plen'y of room to swing a rope!
Plen'y of heart and plen'y of hope.

Oklahoma, where the wind comes sweepin' down the plain,
And the wavin' wheat can sure smell sweet
When the wind comes right behind the rain.
Oklahoma, ev'ry night my honey lamb and I
Sit alone and talk and watch a hawk makin' lazy circles in the sky.

We know we belong to the land
And the land we belong to is grand!
And when we say—Yeeow! A-yip-i-o-ee ay!
We're only sayin' You're doin' fine, Oklahoma! Oklahoma—O.K.!

POPULATION

Population: 3,025,495, twenty-sixth among the states (1980 census)

Population Density: 43 people per sq. mi. (17 people per km²)

Population Distribution: 67 percent of the people live in cities or towns. About 50 percent of Oklahomans live in the Oklahoma City and Tulsa metropolitan areas.

Oklahoma City	403,484
Tulsa	360,919
Lawton	80,054
Norman	68,020
Enid	50,363
Midwest City	49,559
Muskogee	40,011
Stillwater	38,268
Broken Arrow	35,761
Moore	35,063

(Population figures according to 1980 census)

Population Growth: At the time of the Louisiana Purchase, the land that would become Oklahoma supported a modest indigenous Indian population. The forced resettlement of southeastern American Indians increased the population. By 1860, the area had a population of about 80,000 Indians and a number of black slaves. The area was sparsely populated by miners, cowboys, traders, and railroad workers. The land openings brought floods of settlers. About 50,000 arrived in the 1889 land run. The opening of the Cherokee Outlet in 1893 drew an additional 100,000 people. By statehood in 1907, the population had risen to more than 1,400,000. The widespread production of oil brought many oil workers from other parts of the country and also contributed to the state's population growth. However, the Great Depression and the Dust Bowl of the 1930s found Oklahomans leaving the state to find better jobs and better land. The state's continuing poor economy contributed to the population decrease during the 1950s. Industrial growth in the 1960s and 1970s brought a population increase. The population growth rate in the 1970s was 18.2 percent, well above the national average of 11.4 percent.

Year	Population
1890	258,657
1900	790,391
1907	1,414,177
1910	1,657,155
1920	2,028,283
1930	2,396,040
1940	2,336,434
1950	2,233,351
1960	2,328,284
1970	2,559,253
1980	3,025,495

GEOGRAPHY

Borders: States that border Oklahoma are Kansas and Colorado on the north, Arkansas and Missouri on the east, Texas on the south, and Texas and New Mexico on the west.

Highest Point: Black Mesa in the northwest corner of Cimarron County, 4,973 ft. (1,516 m)

Lowest Point: Along the Little River in McCurtain County, 287 ft. (87 m)

Greatest Distances: North to south—230 mi. (370 km)
East to west—464 mi. (747 km)

Area: 69,956 sq. mi. (181,185 km²)

Rank in Area Among the States: Eighteenth

Rivers: Oklahoma's rivers are part of the Mississippi River system and flow in an easterly direction. The state's two major rivers, the Arkansas and the Red, empty into the Mississippi. The Arkansas River flows from northwest to southeast; it enters north-central Oklahoma from Kansas and continues into Arkansas halfway down Oklahoma's eastern border. Major tributaries of the Arkansas River are the Verdigris, Neosho (Grand), Illinois, and Chikaskia rivers flowing from the north, and the Cimarron and Canadian rivers flowing from the west. The Red River forms most of Oklahoma's southern border with Texas. Its major Oklahoma tributaries are the Washita, Blue, Kiamichi, Elm Fork, North Fork, Prairie Dog Town Fork, and Salt Fork rivers.

Lakes: Oklahoma has about one hundred natural lakes and more than two hundred artificial lakes. The artificial lakes, created on Oklahoma's rivers and larger streams, provide hydroelectric power, flood control, irrigation, recreation opportunities, and city water supplies. Lakes in the western part of the state include Great Salt Plains, Fort Supply, Foss, Fort Cobb, Altus, Ellsworth, and Canton. The largest lakes in the south are Lake Texoma and Lake Murray; other southern lakes are Broken Bow Lake, Hugo Lake, Atoka Reservoir, Waurika Lake, and Tom Steed Lake. Important lakes in the northeast are Grand Lake O' the Cherokees, Fort Gibson, Robert S. Kerr, Oologah, Keystone, Tenkiller Ferry, Skiatook, Upper and Lower Spavinaw, Kaw, and Hulah lakes. Lake Eufaula, in east-central Oklahoma, is the largest lake in the state and one of the largest artificial lakes in the world.

Topography: The state of Oklahoma generally slopes from northwest to southwest. The highest point is Black Mesa, on the northwestern tip of the Panhandle. The lowest is in the far southeastern corner, along the Little River.
Three of the nation's major geographic regions meet in Oklahoma: the Interior Plains, the Interior Highlands, and the Coastal Plain. The Interior Plains, including the Great Plains and the Central Lowlands, stretch eastward from the Rocky Mountains. The Interior Highlands slope southward into the state from the Ozark

These rock formations in the High Plains have been named the Wedding Party.

Mountains. Finally, the Coastal Plain reaches northward into the state from the Gulf of Mexico. This geographic meeting provides a great diversity of landscapes in the state.

Within these great geographical divisions, Oklahoma is further divided into ten subregions. The High Plains dominate the westernmost reaches of the state, the Panhandle. This nearly level expanse of land is suitable for grazing and wheat farming.

East of the High Plains, the land slopes downward through the hilly Plains Border region to reach the Central Lowlands, nearly 300 ft. (91 m) lower than the High Plains. The Central Lowlands, which stretch from the state's northern to southern borders, cover most of the state and encompass several geographic features.

In the northwestern part of the state are the Gypsum Hills, a strip of land where a layer of sparkling gypsum caps the low hills.

To the east of the Gypsum Hills are the gently rolling farmlands of the Red Bed Plains, named for the color of the soil beneath the surface.

East of the Red Bed Plains are the low Sandstone Hills, which stretch through the east-central portion of the state from the Red River to the Kansas border. Much of the Sandstone Hills are covered with forests of blackjack and scrub oak; the region also has important oil, gas, and coal deposits.

In the south, two mountainous regions interrupt the Central Lowlands. The Wichita Mountains are granite peaks that rise above the plains in the southwest. The craggy Arbuckle Mountains in the south-central area have eroded into unusual geological formations. These mountainous regions support lumbering and mining as well as limited farming.

113

A winter scene in Martin Park Nature Center, Oklahoma City

Much of the land in the eastern section of the state is part of the Interior Highlands. In the northeast, stretching from the Sandstone Hills to the Arkansas border are the hills, valleys, bluffs, and heavy forests of the Ozark Plateau. Here are small farms that grow primarily fruits and vegetables. The plateau slopes downward to the Arkansas River Valley, an area of rich soil good for farming and cattle grazing. To the south, a finger of the Ouachita Mountains reaches into Oklahoma from Arkansas.

The Red River Plain lies in the southeast section of the state. This region, part of the Coastal Plain, supports a wide variety of farming.

Climate: Oklahoma's climate is generally temperate. Severe storms often strike in spring and summer as warm and cold air masses collide over the state. The north tends to be generally cooler than the rest of the state. The east and the south are more humid, and the west is dry.

In January, the average temperature is 39° F. (4° C). In July, the average temperature is 83° F. (28° C), although temperatures above 100° F. (38° C) are common in all parts of the state during summer. Oklahoma's coldest recorded temperature was -27° F. (-33° C), registered in Vinita in 1905 and Watts in 1930. The highest temperature was 120° F. (49° C), recorded in the summer of 1936 in Alva, Altus, and Poteau.

The state's lightest precipitation is in the west, gradually increasing toward eastern Oklahoma. The Panhandle receives about 15 in. (38 cm) of precipitation a year, while the southeast averages 50 in. (127 cm). This includes rain, snow, and other moisture.

Oklahoma undergoes periods of drought, as well as thunderstorms, hailstorms, blizzards, and tornadoes. Spring and summer tornadoes cause the most damage to people and their property. The tornadoes that struck Woodward in April 1947 killed 101 people and injured more than 1,000.

Cypress trees are among the more than 130 kinds of trees native to Oklahoma.

NATURE

Trees: Longleaf pine, juniper, cottonwood, oak, willow, redbud, hickory, poplar, locust, maple, dogwood, red gum, cypress, ash, elm, pecan, walnut, hackberry, magnolia, blackjack (scrub oak)

Wild Plants: Sagebrush, prickly-pear cactus, shinnery, black-eyed Susan, prairie coneflower, goldenrod, spiderwort, poppy mallow, wild indigo, phlox, verbena, violet, primrose, anemone, wild rose, butterfly weed, and bluestem; gramma, buffalo, Indian, sand, wire, and mesquite grasses

Animals: Deer, armadillos, jackrabbits, cottontails, gray and fox squirrels, prairie dogs, raccoons, coyotes, mink, opossum, gray and red foxes, otters, skunks, antelope, copperhead snakes, cottonmouth snakes, rattlesnakes

Birds: Almost every type of bird between the Mississippi River and the Rocky Mountains nests in Oklahoma. These include blue jays, cardinals, warblers, crows, doves, swallows, meadowlarks, mockingbirds, robins, orioles, scissor-tailed flycatchers, killdeers, English sparrows, red-winged blackbirds, quail, pheasant, wild turkeys, cattle egrets, cowbirds, green and little blue herons, and roadrunners. The world's largest crow roost is in the Fort Cobb Recreation Area northwest of Anadarko. As many as ten million crows descend on the area every October.

Fish: Bass, catfish, buffalo fish, carp, crappie, sunfish, drumfish, paddlefish

GOVERNMENT

Oklahoma's state government, like the federal government, is divided into three branches—executive, legislative, and judicial. The executive branch is responsible for administering the laws. The chief of the executive branch is the governor, who is elected to a four-year term. Governors of Oklahoma may not serve more than two four-year terms in a row. Other executive officials who are elected by the people to four-year terms are the lieutenant governor, the superintendent of public instruction, the attorney general, the auditor and inspector, and the treasurer. The governor appoints several executive officials, including the secretary of state, the finance and revenue chief, the three commissioners of public utilities, and the commissioners of labor, insurance, charities and corrections, and mines.

Oklahoma's legislative, or law-making, branch consists of a 48-member senate and a 101-member house of representatives. Senators are elected for four-year terms in elections held every two years. Representatives serve two-year terms. Regular sessions of the legislature meet every January. The citizens of Oklahoma also may take a direct role in lawmaking. Voters may propose laws and pass them by direct vote in a process called initiative and referendum.

The state government's judicial branch interprets the state laws and tries cases. The major courts are the state supreme court, the court of criminal appeals, and the court of appeals. The nine judges in the supreme court hear appeals of decisions made in the lower civil courts. These judges are elected to six-year terms after first being appointed for one year. The three judges on the court of criminal appeals are also elected to six-year terms. They preside over cases appealed from lower criminal courts. The six court-of-appeals judges are assigned cases by the supreme court. These judges, too, are elected to six-year terms. District, associate, and county judges are elected to four-year terms. Special district judges and municipal judges are appointed to their positions.

Number of Counties: 77

U.S. Representatives: 6

Electoral Votes: 8

Voting Qualifications: Eighteen years of age, United States citizen, and a bona fide resident; voter registration may be canceled for failing to vote in two consecutive general elections.

EDUCATION

Oklahoma's first educational system began in the 1830s, when the Choctaws, Creeks, Chickasaws, Cherokees, and Seminoles began establishing schools and seminaries throughout Indian Territory. The schools were modeled on those in the East, which meant that some Oklahoma Indians were able to read Greek and Latin at a time when many white traders in the area were not able to sign their own

In 1821, Cherokee leader Sequoyah, whose English name was George Gist, invented an alphabet for the Cherokee language.

names. In 1821, Cherokee leader Sequoyah invented a syllabary, or alphabet, for the Cherokee language. As a result, the Cherokee could publish and read a large body of books, newspapers, and other materials in their own language. Widespread public education in Oklahoma began in 1907, the year of statehood. The state's first legislature created a state board of education and instituted free public schools and compulsory attendance for children.

In 1890, the territorial legislature established a teacher-training college, Oklahoma Normal School (now Central State University), in Edmond. In 1892, two more institutions of higher learning were established—the University of Oklahoma at Norman, and Oklahoma Agricultural and Mechanical College (now Oklahoma State University) in Stillwater. These three universities are among the state's twenty-five state-supported institutions of higher learning. These include East Central Oklahoma State University, in Ada; Langston University, in Langston; Northeastern Oklahoma State University, in Tahlequah; and Northwestern Oklahoma State University, in Alva. Approximately 150,000 students are enrolled in Oklahoma's public colleges and universities. Privately run institutions include Oklahoma Baptist University, in Shawnee; Oklahoma City University and Oklahoma Christian College, in Oklahoma City; Bacone College, in Muskogee; Phillips University, in Enid; and the University of Tulsa and Oral Roberts University, in Tulsa. There are about thirty-five institutions of higher learning in Oklahoma and most of these are fully accredited.

School attendance is required for children between the ages of six and seventeen. About 580,000 students attend Oklahoma's more than 1,000 public elementary schools and 800 public middle and secondary schools. Of these, about 330,000 are elementary-school students and 250,000 attend either middle schools or high schools. Nearly 10,000 students attend Oklahoma's more than 80 private elementary and secondary schools.

About 15 percent of Oklahomans twenty-five years of age and over are college graduates. This figure, based on the 1980 census, is higher than the national average.

Salt-storage bins at Catoosa, on the McClellan-Kerr Arkansas River Navigation System

ECONOMY AND INDUSTRY

Principal Products:
Agriculture: Beef cattle, winter wheat, cotton, dairy products, peanuts, hogs, poultry, hay, soybeans, grain sorghum
Manufacturing: Nonelectric machinery, fabricated metal products, electric machinery and equipment, processed food and food products, rubber and plastics products, petroleum and coal products, aircraft, electronic equipment, mobile homes, glass and clay products
Natural Resources: Water, soil, forests, petroleum, natural gas, natural gas liquids, coal, stone, sand, gravel, helium, gypsum, clays, bentonite, pumice, feldspar, iodine, salt, tripoli

Business and Trade: In its early days, Oklahoma's economy depended on agriculture, trapping, and the fur trade. Cattle ranching grew with the age of the cattle drives. The discovery of oil at the turn of the century soon catapulted Oklahoma into one of the nation's largest oil- and gas-producing states. During and after World War II, Oklahoma's manufacturing industries expanded rapidly.

The value of Oklahoma's total output, or gross state product, is more than $50 billion. Manfacturing accounts for about 20 percent of that amount, and wholesale and retail trade about 15 percent. Mining, including fuel production, represents about 11 percent, down from an all-time high of 24 percent in 1981-82.

Finance: Most of the state's expenditures are made through the state's General Revenue Fund. This fund is filled by state taxes, including individual and corporate income taxes, general sales tax, motor fuel taxes, gross production taxes, and taxes on items such as tobacco, insurance, and alcoholic beverages. Oklahoma's various tax sources bring in about $2 billion. The decline in Oklahoma's fuel-production industries in the mid-1980s greatly reduced the state government's income from taxes. About 25 percent of Oklahoma's revenue comes from the federal government. The state's largest expenditures are made for education, public welfare, highways, and hospitals. Since 1939, the state constitution has had a "budget-balancing" amendment that provides a major check on spending.

The drop in oil prices that began in the early 1980s triggered a number of bank failures. Penn Square Bank, an important financial institution in Oklahoma City, closed its doors in July 1982. By the end of 1986, a total of thirty-eight banks had failed. In 1986, the state legislature passed a bill allowing out-of-state banking organizations to acquire Oklahoma banks. This bill may help revive the state's banking system as new capital flows into the state.

Communication: Oklahoma's earliest newspapers were the *Cherokee Messenger*, published in 1843, and the *Cherokee Advocate*, published in both Cherokee and English in 1844. The *Indian Messenger* began in 1876. The Choctaw *Indian Champion* was published in 1883, and the Chickasaws and Creeks also had their own newspapers. Today, about 50 daily and 160 other newspapers are published in Oklahoma. The *Daily Oklahoman, Tulsa Tribune,* and *Tulsa World* have the largest circulations.

About 140 AM and FM radio stations and 20 television stations broadcast from Oklahoma. WKY, the state's first radio station, went on the air in 1921, broadcasting from Oklahoma City. Oklahoma City's KTVY and Tulsa's KOTV were the state's first television stations. Both began broadcasting in 1949.

Transportation: Today, about 110,000 mi. (177,000 km) of roads crisscross the state. Three national interstate highways pass through Oklahoma, all of them intersecting Oklahoma City. Interstate 44 crosses the state from northeast to southwest, passing through both Tulsa and Oklahoma City. Interstate 35 follows a direct north-south route through the state. Interstate 40 crosses Oklahoma from east to west and replaces the legendary Route 66. U.S. Highway 81, a north-south highway just west of Oklahoma City, follows the path of the Chisholm Trail, a famous cattle trail that linked Kansas and Texas. U.S. Highway 69, in eastern Oklahoma, follows a trail called the Trace of the Osage Indians, which in turn followed the Texas Road, one of the earliest trails through Indian Territory into Texas.

Oklahoma's first railroad, the Missouri-Kansas-Texas Railroad, called the *Katy*, was built between 1870 and 1872. Like U.S. Highway 69, it followed the Texas Road. Today, about a dozen rail lines operate over approximately 5,600 mi. (9,000 km) of railroad tracks.

Oklahoma City and Tulsa have the state's major commercial airports, with Oklahoma City's Will Rogers World Airport handling the most air traffic. Fourteen commercial airlines fly into Oklahoma's 150 general-aviation airports.

The McClellan-Kerr Arkansas River Navigation System, opened in 1971, is the state's major commerical waterway.

The Will Rogers Memorial Museum in Claremore

SOCIAL AND CULTURAL LIFE

Museums: Oklahoma's museums reflect the state's diverse cultural and historical heritage. Tulsa's Philbrook Art Center and Thomas Gilcrease Institute of American History and Art are among the finest in the nation. Also in Tulsa is the Fenster Gallery of Jewish Art. In Norman are the University of Oklahoma's Museum of Art and the Oklahoma Museum of Natural History. Oklahoma City is the home of the Oklahoma Art Center and the Oklahoma Science and Arts Foundation Museum. The capital city is also home to the National Cowboy Hall of Fame and Western Heritage Center, which includes the National Rodeo Hall of Fame and the Great Western Performers Hall of Fame. Other Oklahoma museums include the U.S. Army Field Artillery and Fort Sill Museum, and the Museum of the Great Plains in Lawton; the Southern Plains Indian Museum and Crafts Center and the National Hall of Fame for Famous American Indians in Anadarko; and the Will Rogers Memorial Museum in Claremore. The Woolaroc Museum is located in Bartlesville and the Black Kettle Museum is in Cheyenne. The Cherokee National Museum is in Tahlequah, the Creek Indian Museum is in Okmulgee, and the Five Civilized Tribes Museum is in Muskogee. The Pioneer Woman Museum is located in Ponca City.

Maria Tallchief is one of several famous classical ballerinas from Oklahoma.

Libraries: Oklahoma has more than two hundred public libraries. The Oklahoma State Library, founded in Oklahoma City in 1890, is Oklahoma's oldest state-supported library Today it contains Oklahoma's territorial and state archives. The first public library was established in 1901 in Guthrie. The largest public-library systems in the state are the Oklahoma County Library System, with important historical collections, and the Tulsa City-County Library System, with extensive technical collections. Oklahoma has a number of distinguished academic and historical libraries and collections. The University of Oklahoma in Norman houses the DeGolyer collection on the history of science and technology, the Western History Archives, the Bass Business History collection, and the W. B. Bizzell collection of Bibles. The Oklahoma Historical Society Library in Oklahoma City holds the archives of Oklahoma's Indian nations, consisting of some three million documents.

Performing Arts: The performing arts scene in Oklahoma includes both classical and Native American performances. Many cities and towns support local symphony orchestras. The major orchestras are the Oklahoma Symphony in Oklahoma City, the Tulsa Philharmonic, and the Lawton Symphony Orchestra. The annual Tri-State Music Festival, sponsored by Phillips University in Enid, draws young musicians from all over the world. Famous classical ballerinas from Oklahoma—all of Indian ancestry—include Maria Tallchief, Marjorie Tallchief, Yvonne Chouteau, Moscelyne Larkin, and Rozella Hightower. Indian dance exhibitions can be seen at the American Indian Exposition in Anadarko every August and at the many powwows held throughout the state.

Halftime at a University of Oklahoma football game

Sports and Recreation: Oklahoma has no professional football or basketball teams, but fans are rightly proud of the state's college teams. The University of Oklahoma's football Sooners are a powerful running team, with a good defense as well. They are frequent competitors in the Orange Bowl. In the 1986 Orange Bowl, the Sooners beat top-ranked Penn State, and they were ranked number one going into the 1988 Orange Bowl. The Associated Press poll picked them as the nation's top college football team six times: in 1950, 1955, 1956, 1974, 1975, and 1985. Of the twenty-six major college bowl games in which they have played, the Sooners have won eighteen. Coach Barry Switzer holds one of the best winning records in college football. Oklahoma State University's football team, the Cowboys, shares the record for best bowl-game-winning percentage with the University of Southern California. OSU has won seven of its ten bowl games. In college basketball, the University of Oklahoma Sooners are known for their speed and their high scores. They averaged 103.5 points per game in the 1987-88 season, sometimes scoring as high as the 150s. The Sooners made it into the National College Athletic Association (NCAA) Final Four and beat Arizona in the semifinals. Among Oklahoma's distinguished individual athletes are gymnast Bart Connors, an Olympic gold-medal winner, and wrestler John Smith, the 1987 world champion. Over the years, Oklahomans Warren Spahn, Mickey Mantle, and Johnny Bench have added excitement to baseball's World Series. Jim Thorpe, America's legendary Olympic athlete, was an Oklahoman.

122

Oklahoma's lakes and rivers provide many recreation opportunities for residents and out-of-state visitors. With more than two hundred artificially created lakes, the state has excellent facilities for boating, water skiing, and fishing. Lake Eufaula and Lake Texoma are the largest in the state. Other popular lake sites are Grand Lake O' the Cherokees, Fort Gibson Lake, Tenkiller Ferry Lake, and Keystone Lake. Oklahoma has several resorts that offer tennis courts, golf courses, hotels, cottages, and restaurants; they include Lake Texoma Resort, Lake Murray Resort, Western Hills Guest Ranch, Quartz Mountain Resort, and Roman Nose Resort.

Most of Oklahoma's thirty-two state parks are situated alongside its lakes. There are also twenty-eight state recreation areas and forty-eight state wildlife management areas. In Alabaster Caverns State Park, near Freedom, is the world's largest gypsum cave that is open to the public. Robbers Cave State Park near Wilburn offers hiking and fishing areas, as well as an opportunity to visit several caves that were once hideouts for robbers. In the Panhandle's Black Mesa State Park are Black Mesa, the state's highest point, and dinosaur excavation sites. Quartz Mountain State Park on Lake Altus is noted for its scenic canyons and mountains.

Both the Oklahoma City Zoo and the Tulsa Zoological Park are accredited by the American Association of Zoological Parks and Aquariums. The Oklahoma City Zoo houses many rare animals. Its marine arena—Aquaticus—holds entertaining dolphin shows daily. Horseback riding and horse racing are popular recreations in Oklahoma. Many cities and towns offer horse shows, rodeos, polo matches, and horse-farm tours. Eight of the state parks rent horses for riding on park equestrian trails. Blue Ribbon Downs in Sallisaw and Remington Park in Oklahoma City are the major horse-racing tracks. For rugged nature lovers, there are dozens of official hiking and backpacking trails.

Historic Sites and Landmarks:

Sequoyah's Home, near Sallisaw, was constructed in 1829. The preserved log cabin was the home of the inventor of the Cherokee alphabet.

Spiro Mounds Archaeological State Park, in east-central Oklahoma, is an excavation site supervised by the University of Oklahoma Archaeology Department. Artifacts found in the burial mounds give a fascinating picture of Oklahoma's early Mound Builder culture.

U.S. Army Field Artillery and Fort Sill Museum, in Lawton, is a national historic landmark that features two centuries' worth of American field artillery. The museum complex includes Geronimo's guardhouse, the fort's old stone corral, and the graves of Geronimo and other Indian chiefs.

Washita Battlefield, northwest of Cheyenne, is the site of the 1868 battle between George Custer and Cheyenne Indians under Chief Black Kettle. Custer's troops killed or wounded more than one hundred Cheyenne men, women, and children in the surprise attack.

Actor John Wayne's collection of elaborately costumed Kachina dolls is on display at the National Cowboy Hall of Fame and Western Heritage Center in Oklahoma City.

Other Interesting Places to Visit:

Arbuckle Wilderness, in south-central Oklahoma, features a scenic drive through the Arbuckle Mountains. Hundreds of exotic wild animals—some from other continents—roam free in the wilderness. They include llamas, yaks, giraffes, lions, ostriches, and kangaroos.

Creek National Tribal Complex, in Okmulgee, includes a large, circular, mound-shaped building. While the mound recalls the ancient Creek home-building tradition, it also houses the modern-day Creeks' tribal business offices.

Heavener Runestone State Park, near Heavener, features the massive Heavener Runestone, with alphabet markings that date back to A.D. 1012. The inscriptions are believed to have been carved by Norse explorers.

Chickasaw National Recreation Area, in south-central Oklahoma, includes the former Platt National Park, with its mineral springs, and the Arbuckle Recreation Area, with swimming, boating, fishing, and camping facilities.

National Cowboy Hall of Fame and Western Heritage Center, in Oklahoma City, holds the world's largest collection of Western Americana. It includes the National Rodeo Hall of Fame and the Great Western Performers Hall of Fame. Actor John Wayne donated his kachina doll collection and other memorabilia to the museum.

Oklahoma Aviation and Space Hall of Fame, in Oklahoma City, has many hands-on exhibits and artifacts that illustrate the history of aviation and space exploration. Special exhibits honor Oklahoma aviators and astronauts.

Ouachita National Forest, in southeastern Oklahoma, extends into Arkansas. This sprawling mountainous forest features scenic drives, hiking trails, lakes and ridges, and areas for camping and picnicking.

Pioneer Woman Statue and Museum, in Ponca City, features a bronze statue honoring the pioneer women who helped settle the West. The museum displays antique household furniture and costumes from the pioneer era.

Tsa-La-Gi Ancient Village, in Tahlequah, is an authentic re-creation of a seventeenth-century Cherokee village. Cherokees in the village demonstrate their ancestors' special skills, crafts, and everyday ways of life.

Wichita Mountains National Wildlife Refuge, near Lawton, maintains herds of bison and longhorn cattle. Elk, deer, and prairie dogs can also be seen.

Will Rogers Memorial, in Claremore, contains personal possessions of the beloved entertainer as well as photographs, trophies, his saddle collection, and letters from famous people. The 178-seat theater shows films daily.

Woolaroc Museum, near Bartlesville, was once the ranch house of oil magnate Frank Phillips. It features thousands of historical exhibits. Buffalo, deer, peacocks, ostriches, and other wildlife roam the surrounding grounds.

IMPORTANT DATES

c. 8000 B.C. — Hunters from Clovis and Folsom cultures track game in plains of Oklahoma

c. A.D. 800 — Mound Builder culture flourishes in eastern Oklahoma; it reaches its peak between 1200 and 1350

Early 1000s — Norsemen explore the Arkansas River Valley, leaving inscriptions in runestones in Heavener, Poteau, and Shawnee vicinities

1541 — Francisco Vásquez de Coronado crosses western Oklahoma in search of riches; he claims the western half of the Mississippi River Valley for Spain; Hernando De Soto explores eastern Oklahoma

1542 — Hernando De Soto dies near what is now Little Rock, Arkansas, after exploring along the eastern border of Oklahoma

1601 — Explorer Juan de Oñate encounters Oklahoma's Antelope Hills while exploring the Southwest

1650 — Don Diego de Castillo spends six months prospecting for gold and silver in Oklahoma's Wichita Mountains

1682 — René-Robert Cavelier, Sieur de la Salle, claims the entire lower Mississippi River Valley (including Oklahoma) for France and names the territory Louisiana in honor of the French monarch, Louis XIV

1714 — French trader Juchereau de St. Denis sails up the Red River, becoming the first Frenchman to actually see Oklahoma

1719 — Bernard de la Harpe explores the Red River region in the southeast part of the state, continuing up through Muskogee, to Haskell; Claude du Tisne visits Pawnee villages near present-day Chelsea

1741 — Fabry de la Bruyere camps on the Canadian River while exploring the Arkansas River system

1759 — Spaniards under Diego Parilla attack French settlements of San Bernardo and San Teodoro

1762 — France cedes Louisiana (including Oklahoma) to Spain

1800 — Spain cedes Louisiana (including Oklahoma) back to France

1802 — The federal government makes an agreement with the state of Georgia to move Creek and Cherokee Indians to western lands

1803 — The United States purchases the Louisiana Territory, including Oklahoma, from France; President Thomas Jefferson proposes that land belonging to Indians in eastern states be exchanged for land in the District of Louisiana

1804 — The District of Louisiana is put under the jurisdiction of Indiana territorial governor William Henry Harrison; Congress initiates the first resettlements of southeastern Indians

1806 — Captain Richard Sparks sets out to follow the Red River to its source; Lieutenant James Wilkinson explores the Arkansas River

1811 — George Sibley's expedition crosses the Great Salt Plains

1812 — Lands west of the Mississippi River, including Oklahoma, are named Missouri Territory

1817 — Treaty exchanges part of Cherokee ancestral lands for lands west of the Mississippi River in the Arkansas and White river valleys

1819 — Arkansas and most of Oklahoma become Arkansas Territory; naturalist Thomas Nuttall studies Oklahoma's wildlife and geology and writes about them in his *Journal of Travels in the Arkansas Territory*

1820 — Choctaws in Mississippi sign the Treaty of Doak's Stand, exchanging ancestral lands for lands north of the Red River

1824 — Forts Gibson and Towson are founded

1826 — Creeks in Alabama sign removal treaty, agreeing to move to western lands

1828 — Cherokees resettled in Arkansas sign treaty to move again — farther west

1830 — Indian Removal Act is passed by Congress

1832 — American writer Washington Irving tours Oklahoma and writes of his experiences in *A Tour of the Prairies*; Mississippi Chickasaws, Florida Seminoles, and Georgia Creeks sign removal treaties

1834 — Congress declares most of present-day eastern Oklahoma to be Indian Territory; General Henry Leavenworth and Colonel Henry Dodge persuade Plains Indians of western Oklahoma to accept the influx of Indians from eastern Oklahoma as well as the eastern United States

1835 — Georgia Cherokees sign removal treaty

1838-39 — Eastern Indians, primarily Cherokees, make the bitter winter trek to Indian Territory in what becomes known as the Trail of Tears

1861 — Indian Territory joins the Confederacy after the Civil War begins

1865 — Brigadier General Stand Watie surrenders to the Union army

1866 — The Five Civilized Tribes sign Reconstruction treaties

1872 — Oklahoma's first commercial coal mine is opened; railroad first crosses what is now the state of Oklahoma

1879 — David L. Payne organizes the "Boomers"

1889 — The Unassigned Lands are opened for settlement in the great Land Run of April 22; Edward Byrd drills Oklahoma's first oil-producing well near Chelsea

1890 — Indian Territory is divided into the twin territories of Oklahoma Territory and Indian Territory; the Oklahoma Organic Act sets up Oklahoma's territorial government; the Panhandle is annexed

1891 — Iowa, Sac and Fox, Shawnee, and Potawatomi lands are opened for white settlement

1892—Cheyenne and Arapaho lands are opened for settlement

1893—The Dawes Commission is established to negotiate division of tribal lands and reallotment of the lands on an individual basis; the Cherokee Outlet is opened for settlement

1894—Apache chief Geronimo surrenders to the U.S. Army; he is later imprisoned at Fort Sill

1895—Kickapoo lands are opened

1896—Greer County is annexed to Oklahoma after the U.S. Supreme Court declares Texas's claim invalid

1897—Frank Phillips drills Oklahoma's first commercial oil well in Bartlesville

1901—Wichita, Caddo, Comanche, Kiowa, and Apache lands are settled by lottery; the Red Fork oil field is discovered near Tulsa

1905—Tulsa's Glenn Pool oil field is discovered

1906—The Big Pasture lands are opened for sale to settlers

1907—Oklahoma becomes the forty-sixth state of the Union

1910—The state capital is moved from Guthrie to Oklahoma City

1923—Governor John Walton is impeached

1928—One of the world's richest oil fields is discovered near Oklahoma City

1929—Governor Henry Johnston is impeached

1930—The Dust Bowl drives many Oklahomans out of the state

1943—Robert S. Kerr becomes Oklahoma's first native-born governor

1953—Oklahoma's first turnpike, the Turner Turnpike, is completed

1959—Prohibition, in effect in Oklahoma since 1907, is repealed

1963—Henry Bellmon becomes Oklahoma's first Republican governor

1964—Federal aerospace industry expenditures in Oklahoma reach $600 million

1971—The McClellan-Kerr Arkansas River Navigation System opens

1982—The drop in world oil prices causes a decline in Oklahoma's economy

IMPORTANT PEOPLE

Carl Albert (1908-   ), born in McAlester; attorney and politician; congressman from Oklahoma (1947-76); Democratic Whip (1955-62); House majority leader (1962-71); Speaker of the U.S. House of Representatives (1970-76)

William Bennett Bizzell (1874-1944), educator and author; first president of the University of Oklahoma (1925-41); helped establish the University of Oklahoma Press (1928)

Jesse Chisholm (1805-1868), Cherokee Indian trader; his route north through Indian Territory to his Wichita, Kansas trading post (the Chisholm Trail) became the favorite of cattle drivers in the 1860s and 1870s

Jean Pierre Chousreau (1758-1849), fur trader and pioneer; established the first permanent white settlement in Oklahoma (1796)

Yvonne Chouteau (1929-   ), born in Oklahoma City; classical ballerina; at fourteen became the youngest American ever admitted into the Ballet Russe de Monte Carlo

Leroy Gordon Cooper, Jr. (1927-   ), born in Shawnee; one of the country's seven original astronauts (1959), and the first to make two space flights that orbited the earth

Francisco Vásquez de Coronado (1510-1554), Spanish explorer; crossed the state in 1541 in search of legendary riches

Angie Debo (1890-1988), historian, "first lady of Oklahoma history"; arrived in Oklahoma Territory by covered wagon; wrote thirteen books, among them *Oklahoma, Foot-Loose and Fancy-Free, The Rise and Fall of the Choctaw Nation,* and *Geronimo: The Man, His Time, His Place*

Bill Doolin (1858-1896), outlaw; head of the notorious Doolin Gang; killed in an ambush by lawman Marshal Heck Thomas; buried in Guthrie

Ralph Waldo Ellison (1914-   ), born in Oklahoma City; author and educator; his novel *Invisible Man*   (1952) is a classic story of the black experience in America

Owen K. Garriott (1930-   ), born in Enid, astronaut; member of the Skylab space project

Geronimo (1829-1909), Apache warrior; led attacks on settlers in the Southwest during the 1870s and 1880s; imprisoned at Fort Sill from 1894 until his death

Thomas Gilcrease (1890-1962), oil magnate; donated his private art collection, which became the basis for Tulsa's Gilcrease Institute of American History and Art

CARL ALBERT

RALPH ELLISON

OWEN K. GARRIOTT

GERONIMO

WOODY GUTHRIE

WASHINGTON IRVING

MICKEY MANTLE

ERNEST W. MARLAND

Woodrow Wilson (Woody) Guthrie (1912-1967), born in Okemah; songwriter, musician; published more than one thousand songs of hard times, social injustice, and the beauty of the land; wrote "This Land is Your Land"; influenced folk singers such as Bob Dylan; wrote his autobiography, *Bound for Glory*, in 1943

Washington Irving (1783-1859), American author; specialized in tales of American folk life and folkways; wrote *A Tour of the Prairies* after his 1830s travels in Oklahoma

Karl Jansky (1905-1950), born in Norman; radio research engineer; first to detect radio waves from space, laying the foundation for the science of radio astronomy

John M. Johansen (1916-   ), architect; designed the Mummer's Theater (1970), now Stage Center in Oklahoma's Myriad complex; the award-winning structure revolutionized architectural concepts

Maybelle Kennedy (1891-   ), Pawhuska banker and rancher; assistant treasurer of the United States under President Harry S. Truman (1952-53)

Robert Samuel Kerr (1893-1963), born near Ada; politician; first of the state's governors (1943-47) to have been born in Oklahoma; U.S. senator (1949-63) who helped procure federal appropriations for such state projects as the McClellan-Kerr Arkansas River Navigation Project

Gordon William "Pawnee Bill" Lillie (1860-1942), performer; owned a ranch near Pawnee; member of Buffalo Bill's Wild West Show; started the Pawnee Bill Show in 1888; the show, featuring his wife, May, toured the world until 1913

Mickey Mantle (1931-   ), born in Spavinaw; professional baseball player; center fielder with the New York Yankees for eighteen years; played 2,401 games, more than any other Yankee; elected to the baseball Hall of Fame in 1974

Wilma Mankiller (1945-   ), born in Rocky Mountain; first woman to serve as Principal Chief of the Cherokee Nation (1985-   )

Ernest W. Marland (1874-1941), oilman and politician; governor (1935-39); founder of the Marland Oil Company in Ponca City, which later merged with Continental Oil Company; his mansion in Ponca City is known as the "palace on the prairie"; gave the Pioneer Woman Statue, one of the largest bronze statues in the world, as a gift to Oklahoma and a tribute to women all over the world

N. Scott Momaday (1934-   ), writer; received the 1969 Pulitzer Prize in fiction for *House Made of Dawn*

Zack Mulhall (1847-1931), Oklahoma Territory rancher and performer; operated a touring Wild West Show starring his daughter Lucille, the "World's First Cowgirl" (1900-15)

William Henry "Alfalfa Bill" Murray (1869-1956), politician; president of Oklahoma's constitutional convention; governor (1931-35); known for his folksy character and sense of humor, as well as for his toughness during the difficult depression era

Thomas Nuttall (1786-1859), botanist and ornithologist; wrote *Journal of Travels in the Arkansas Territory*, the first important scientific study of Oklahoma's plant life and geology

David L. Payne (1836-1884), soldier, pioneer, and adventurer; served in the Union army and in the Kansas legislature; dynamic leader of the "Boomer" movement to open Oklahoma land for white settlement

Frank Phillips (1873-1950), oilman and philanthropist; drilled Oklahoma's first commercial oil well near Bartlesville (1897); founded Phillips Petroleum Company; founded Woolaroc Museum near Bartlesville

Waite Phillips (1883-1964), oil magnate brother of oilman Frank Phillips; turned his Italian Renaissance villa in Tulsa into the Philbrook Art Center and donated it, with an impressive collection of classical artworks, to the city of Tulsa

Zebulon Pike (1779-1813), soldier and explorer; directed by General James Wilkinson to follow the Arkansas River to its source; traveled up the Arkansas River through Oklahoma to the Rocky Mountains; Pike's Peak, the peak he tried unsuccessfully to climb, was named in his honor

William R. Pogue (1930-   ), born in Okemah; astronaut; shares the American record for longest space flight (eighty-four days)

Lynn Riggs (1899-1954), playwright; his play *Green Grow the Lilacs* was the basis for the Rodgers and Hammerstein musical *Oklahoma!*

Oral Roberts (1918-   ), born near Ada; evangelist, clergyman, and author; served as a minister in Enid and organized evangelist crusade teams that travel around the world; founded Oral Roberts University in Tulsa

Alice Mary Robertson (1854-1931), born in Muskogee; educator, social worker, and politician; member of U.S. House of Representatives (1921-23)

Will Rogers (1879-1935), born in Oologah; entertainer and humorist; began as a trick roper in Wild West shows; performed in vaudeville; in 1916 starred in the Ziegfeld Follies; appeared in seventy-one Hollywood films; died in a plane crash while flying with aviator Wiley Post

Sequoyah (1770?-1843), Cherokee leader; came to Indian Territory during the Indian removal of 1829; created an eighty-four-letter syllabary, or alphabet, for the Cherokee language, enabling the nation to publish books, newspapers, and educational materials in the Cherokee language

ZEBULON PIKE

WILLIAM R. POGUE

WILL ROGERS

SEQUOYAH

MARIA TALLCHIEF

JIM THORPE

Thomas P. Stafford (1930-   ), born in Weatherford; astronaut; has flown four space missions, including a trip to the moon; commanded the Apollo-Soyuz joint mission

Belle Starr (1848-1889), outlaw in Indian Territory; accused of robbery, arson, horse stealing, and bootlegging; sentenced to a federal prison in 1882 by Judge Isaac Parker, the ''hanging judge''; later paroled; mysteriously murdered on her homestead near Eufaula

George Steele (1839-1942), first territorial governor of Oklahoma Territory (1890-91)

Maria Tallchief (1925-   ), born in Fairfax; ballerina; among the first American classical ballerinas to achieve international fame; danced with the Ballet Russe de Monte Carlo (1942-47); prima ballerina of the New York City Ballet (1947-60); founder, Chicago City Ballet (1979)

James Francis (Jim) Thorpe (1887-1953), born near Prague; international sports hero; won gold medals in both the pentathlon and the decathlon in the 1912 Olympics in Stockholm, Sweden; in 1950 was voted the greatest athlete of the half-century

Jerome Tiger (1941-1967), artist; his innovative painting style ranked him as one of the country's most respected artists

Stand Watie (1806-1871), Cherokee tribal leader; moved from Georgia to Oklahoma during the 1838 Cherokee removal; led the Cherokee Mounted Rifles regiment of the Confederate army; promoted to brigadier general in 1864

Charles Banks Wilson (1918-   ), artist; his portraits of famous Oklahomans and murals of scenes from Oklahoma history decorate the state capitol rotunda in Oklahoma City

GOVERNORS

Charles N. Haskell	1907-1911	Johnston Murray	1951-1955
Lee Cruce	1911-1915	Raymond Gary	1955-1959
Robert L. Williams	1915-1919	J. Howard Edmondson	1959-1963
James B. A. Robertson	1919-1923	George P. Nigh	1963
John C. Walton	1923	Henry L. Bellmon	1963-1967
Martin E. Trapp	1923-1927	Dewey F. Bartlett	1967-1971
Henry S. Johnston	1927-1929	David Hall	1971-1975
William J. Holloway	1929-1931	David L. Boren	1975-1979
William H. Murray	1931-1935	George Nigh	1979-1987
Ernest W. Marland	1935-1939	Henry L. Bellmon	1987-
Leon C. Phillips	1939-1943		
Robert S. Kerr	1943-1947		
Roy J. Turner	1947-1951		

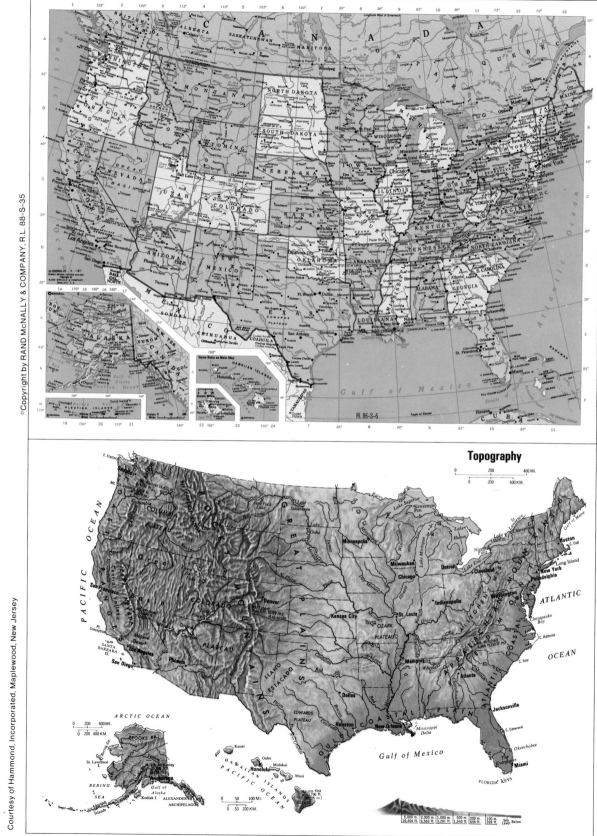

© Copyright by RAND McNALLY & COMPANY, R.L. 88-S-35

Courtesy of Hammond, Incorporated, Maplewood, New Jersey

Topography

MAP KEY

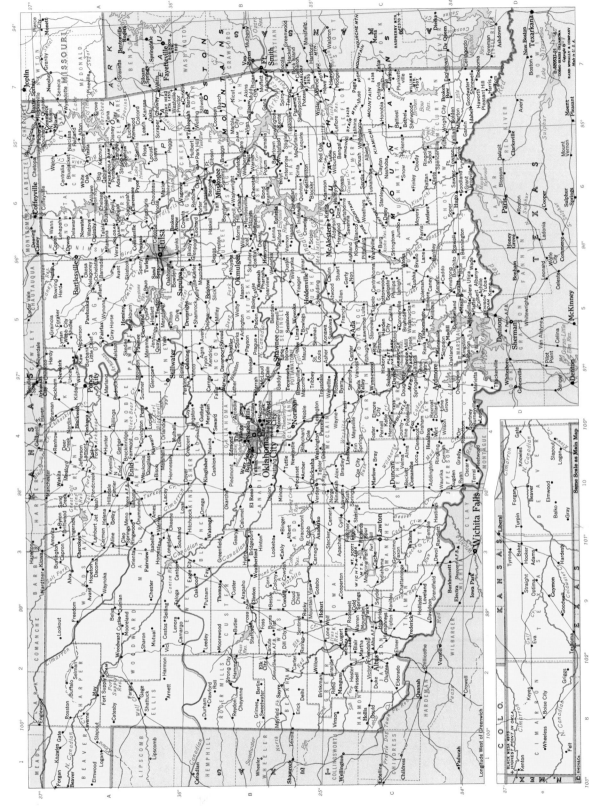

©Copyright by RAND McNALLY & COMPANY, R.L. 88-S-35

Lambert Conformal Conic Projection

✹ HAY	☺ VEGETABLES	🐖 HOGS
🌾 OATS	🥔 POTATOES	🐑 SHEEP
⚘ CORN	🌳 FRUIT	⛏ OIL
🌾 WHEAT	🍇 GRAPES	🔥 NATURAL GAS
🌾 BARLEY	🥐 PECANS	⚗ HELIUM
🌾 SORGHUMS	🥜 PEANUTS	✕ MINING
🌸 COTTON	🐓 POULTRY	FOREST PRODUCTS
🌾 BROOMCORN	🥛 DAIRY PRODUCTS	🌷 NURSERY PRODUCTS
🌿 SOYBEANS	🐄 BEEF	

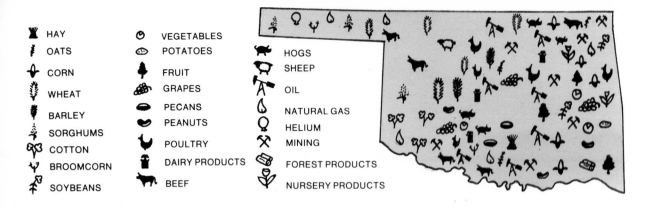

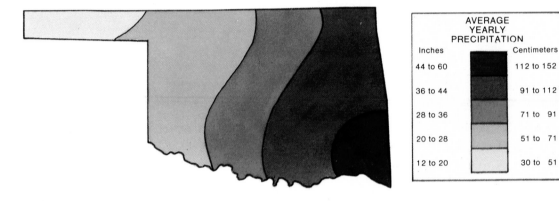

AVERAGE YEARLY PRECIPITATION

Inches		Centimeters
44 to 60		112 to 152
36 to 44		91 to 112
28 to 36		71 to 91
20 to 28		51 to 71
12 to 20		30 to 51

POPULATION DENSITY

Number of persons per square kilometer		Number of persons per square mile
more than 20		more than 50
10 to 20		25 to 50
4 to 10		10 to 25
Less than 4		Less than 10

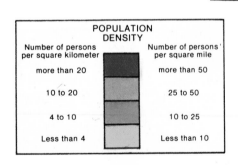

MAJOR HIGHWAYS

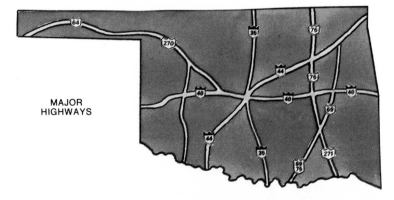

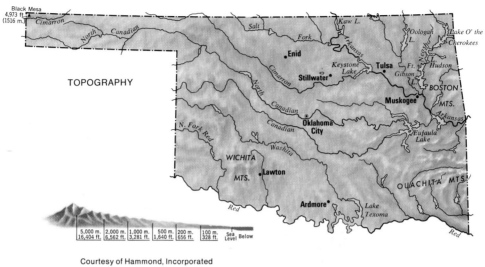

TOPOGRAPHY

Black Mesa
4,973 ft.
(1516 m.)

| 5,000 m. 16,404 ft. | 2,000 m. 6,562 ft. | 1,000 m. 3,281 ft. | 500 m. 1,640 ft. | 200 m. 656 ft. | 100 m. 328 ft. | Sea Level | Below |

Courtesy of Hammond, Incorporated

Maplewood, New Jersey

COUNTIES

A night view of Tulsa

INDEX

Page numbers that appear in boldface type indicate illustrations.

The Anadarko oil field basin, Elk City

Picture Identifications

Front cover: A view of Tulsa with an oil refinery in the foreground
Back cover: Turner Falls, in the Arbuckle Mountains near Davis
Pages 2-3: Bison at the Wichita Mountains National Wildlife Refuge
Page 6: Red Rock Canyon State Park, Caddo County
Page 8: Antelope Hills, Roger Mills County
Pages 16-17: Montage of Oklahomans
Page 27: René-Robert Cavelier, Sieur de La Salle, landing in the Gulf of Mexico in 1865 on his return to the region he had claimed for France.
Pages 36-37: Emigrants to the American West
Page 48: The 1891 Oklahoma land run
Pages 60-61: Oklahoma City skyline
Pages 70-71: Oklahoma State Capitol, Oklahoma City
Pages 80-81: Stage Center at Myriad Gardens, Oklahoma City
Page 81 (inset): *Fast Baller,* a Jerome Tiger painting of a moment of action in the game of stickball
Page 94: An Oklahoma oil well
Page 94 (inset): Great Salt Plains Lake at sunset
Page 108: Montage showing the state flag, the state bird (scissor-tailed flycatcher), the state rock (barite rose rock), and the state wildflower (Indian blanket)

About the Author

Ann Heinrichs was born and raised in Fort Smith, Arkansas, and as a child enjoyed many family forays into Oklahoma. Now a free-lance writer and editor living in Chicago, Ms. Heinrichs has worked for such educational publishers as Encyclopaedia Britannica, World Book Encyclopedia, and Science Research Associates. As a music critic and feature writer, her articles have appeared in a number of magazines. For Childrens Press she has authored *I Can Be a Chef, The Hopi,* and, in the *America the Beautiful* series, *Oklahoma* and *Arkansas.*

Picture Acknowledgments

H. Armstrong Roberts: Pages 50, 75, 94 (background picture), 131 (bottom); ©Camerique: Front cover, pages 60-61; ©T. Ulrich: Pages 2-3; ©Abernathy: Page 5; ©W. Metzen: Pages 10, 15, 21 (left), 70-71, 77 (both pictures), 108 (bottom right), 120, 141; ©R. Krubner: Pages 78, 86, 104
Southern Stock Photos: Back cover; ©Vic Pakis: Page 6
©**Jim Argo:** Pages 4, 13, 16 (top left, bottom left, bottom right), 17 (top left, bottom right), 19, 21 (top right), 22 (right), 30, 31 (inset), 57, 68 (right), 84, 91, 92 (left), 93, 98, 100 (both pictures), 106, 107, 122
©**David Halpern:** Pages 8, 22 (left), 55 (color picture), 138
Oklahoma Tourism and Recreation Department: Fred W. Marvel: Pages 12, 21 (bottom right), 41, 52, 68 (left), 92 (right), 96, 102, 113, 114
Root Resources: ©Lia Munson: Page 14; ©Mary and Loren Root: Page 108 (bottom left); ©Kitty Kohout: Page 108 (tree); ©Vera Bradshaw: Page 118
©**Porterfield/Chickering:** Pages 16 (middle left), 25 (bottom right), 74, 83
PictureWorks: ©Rita J. DeDominick: Pages 16 (top right), 17 (middle left); ©Howard Robson: Page 17 (bottom left); ©Sandy Snyder: Page 24
©**James P. Rowan:** Page 25 (top)
Photri: Pages 25 (bottom left), 66, 110, 121; ©M.S. Meyers: Page 94 (inset)
The Granger Collection, New York: Pages 27, 34, 36-37, 39, 48, 51, 53 (right), 67 (left), 117
No Man's Land Museum, Oklahoma Historical Society: Page 29
©**Ann Heinrichs:** Page 31 (left)
Wide World Photos: Pages 53 (bottom left), 129 (top), 130 (Guthrie, Mantle, Marland), 131 (Pogue, Rogers), 132 (both pictures)
The Bettmann Archive: Pages 32, 67 (right), 129 (bottom), 131 (top)
UPI/Bettmann Newsphotos: Page 129 (Ellison and Garriott)
North Wind Picture Archives: Pages 43, 47
National Gallery of Art, Washington, Paul Mellon Collection: Page 44
The Philbrook Museum of Art, Tulsa, Oklahoma: Page 45
Archives & Manuscripts Division, Oklahoma Historical Society: Page 53 (top left), 55 (inset), 63
©**Diana O. Rasche 1988:** Page 79
©**SuperStock International:** Pages 80-81
Five Civilized Tribes Museum: Pages 81 (inset), 85
©**David G. Fitzgerald:** Pages 88, 101, 103, 115
Tom Stack & Associates: ©R.C. Simpson: Page 108 (top right)
R/C Photo Agency: ©Richard L. Capps: Page 124
Library of Congress: Page 130 (Irving)
Len W. Meents: Maps on pages 96, 98, 100, 102, 104, 106, 136
Courtesy Flag Research Center, Winchester, Massachusetts 01890: Flag on page 108

976.6
HEI

Heinrichs, Ann
Oklahoma

DATE DUE

JAN 3 0	OCT 28	NOV 23	
FEB	NOV 13		
FEB 8	fac		
FEB 1 6	MAR 18	DEC 1 3	
MAR	FEB 29	JAN 11	
MAR 2 9	MAR 14	JAN 9	
FEB 1	OCT 7	MAR 1 5	
FEB 6		MAR 22	
JAN 1 4	OCT 17	APR 5	
MAR 24	OCT 12	FEB 14	
O 5	NOV 9		

pink mark on p. 9 — 12/94

DEMCO